Police Family Liais(

Police Family Liaison

Duncan McGarry
and
Kevin Smith

OXFORD
UNIVERSITY PRESS

OXFORD
UNIVERSITY PRESS

Great Clarendon Street, Oxford OX2 6DP

Oxford University Press is a department of the University of Oxford.
It furthers the University's objective of excellence in research, scholarship, and education by publishing worldwide in

Oxford NewYork

Auckland Cape Town Dar es Salaam Hong Kong Karachi
Kuala Lumpur Madrid Melbourne Mexico City Nairobi
New Delhi Shanghai Taipei Toronto

With offices in

Argentina Austria Brazil Chile Czech Republic France Greece
Guatemala Hungary Italy Japan Poland Portugal Singapore
South Korea Switzerland Thailand Turkey Ukraine Vietnam

Published in the United States
by Oxford University Press Inc., NewYork

First published 2011

British Library Cataloguing in Publication Data

Data available

Library of Congress Cataloging in Publication Data

Library of Congress Control Number: 2010942943

Typeset by Glyph International, Bangalore, India
Printed in Great Britain
on acid-free paper by
CPI Antony Rowe, Chippenham, Wiltshire

ISBN 978-0-19-921408-2

10 9 8 7 6 5 4 3 2 1

Foreword

It is an honour to write these words in an important book for Duncan McGarry and Kevin Smith. The three of us had been part of a policing team in 1998 tasked with attempting to put right a catastrophic investigation. The Stephen Lawrence Inquiry into a racist murder five years earlier caused a tectonic shift in police work that this book describes. The discussions we had initially and in the weeks, months and years that have followed did much to put right what had gone wrong and helped avoid many more disasters. With many others, Duncan and Kevin's work formed a foundation for a strategy that provided some of the responses to at least a quarter of the Stephen Lawrence Inquiry's seventy recommendations when they came in 1999 and did much to satisfy the then Home Secretary, Jack Straw's action plan a month later. Most of this material arrived on the desks of our team, specifically into the in and out trays of Detective Constable Duncan McGarry and concerned family liaison the subject of this important ground breaking book.

We have always had family liaison officers on every murder squad I had worked on over the preceding 30 years. What Duncan, Kevin, Ron Cuthbertson, Dave Field, and others were advocating was to prepare a trained cadre of specialist skilled members of a new discipline to help families, secondary victims, communities. They saw them as like firearms officers or scenes of crime specialists. They explained a strategy, a guidance manual, a program for teaching and preparing officers for the difficult role they were to perform at the beginning of the twenty-first century. From the outset they paid tribute to the pioneering work in this field of Avon and Somerset Police Service (we subsequently discovered that An Garda Siochana in Ireland had thought through these issues three years before). It was a BGO, a blinding glimpse of the obvious! They explored the psychology and pressures experienced by families and their communities, the welfare and information needs of relatives in differing family structures and cultures. But they also identified the requirements of the specialist officers themselves. I should have been acutely aware of this latter task, as an FLO had sought my advice before the public inquiry. All that I had said, I subsequently decided, had been of little or no value. A few minutes with Duncan, Dave, Kevin or Ron, or indeed this timely and detailed book would have been of infinitely greater value, predictive, relevant and supportive of both the families and the officers. What was an issue for the family was an issue for us, and particularly for the FLOs. Mrs and Mr Lawrence identified to the public inquiry, matters which would lie at the heart of reforms described here and of lasting benefit to every victim's family. That is why this book is so important.

Duncan, Kevin and others helped us explore and codify the investigative tasks of the FLOs. We examined the judgements, decisions and records required by families, communities, us, lawyers and the criminal justice system. These developments led to a higher degree of sensitivity to the needs and attitudes not just of victims, families, communities but also pressure groups, networks, institutions, supporters, and the media.

We needed mechanisms that would change all this thinking into an organisational change program. Duncan, Kevin, and others led the preparation of an investigative tactical doctrine the latest iteration of which is in this book heralding cultural changes that became a lifeline in the difficult days ahead. This group was a steel on which the service sharpened our ideas and arguments about what had to be reformed and why. When the Public Inquiry reported we had a methodology ready. It was then that Duncan and Kevin began a rigorous systematic expansion and embedding of the family liaison philosophy that has continued to the publication of this book. The work undertaken, nationwide and internationally has been momentous and influential in areas of policing and wider policy.

Robert Peel had said, two centuries before, that he wanted his new police to be 'civil and obliging'. The investigative skills described in this book reinvigorated and refreshed his ideals for a committed and co operative workforce giving them an increased set of skills. Though junior in rank the FLO is a traditionalist, leader but also innovator in policing.

Nothing gives me more satisfaction, looking back at the days with Duncan and Kevin and all those others, when in the aftermath of some current murder trial, watching a family representative on the television news thank the investigative team of detectives and then single out their family liaison officers for praise. Shadowy in their background I can see Mr and Mrs Lawrence, Avon and Somerset officers, An Garda Siochana, many people involved in this aspect of policing, and of course Duncan McGarry and Kevin Smith. This book will enhance that police work.

John G.D. Grieve CBE. QPM.
Senior Research Fellow, University of Portsmouth.
Professor Emeritus, London Metropolitan University.

References:

Hall N. Grieve J. Savage S. P. 2009. *Policing and the Legacy of Lawrence*. Devon. Willan.

Savage S. 2007. *Police Reform. Forces for change*. Oxford. Oxford University Press.

TSO 1999a *Stephen Lawrence Inquiry*. Report by Sir William Macpherson. London. The Stationery Office. February 1999.

TSO 1999b *Stephen Lawrence Inquiry*. Home Secretary's Action Plan. London. The Stationery Office. March 1999.

Acknowledgments

The authors would like to thank Dr Anne Eyre for her commitment to and support for police family liaison and for giving them access to her research.

Contents

Special Features

This book contains several special features that it is hoped will make it more helpful to the reader. These are defined and explained below.

Key Points

Where it has been felt appropriate to reinforce an important or pertinent point which has been covered within the text of the chapters, a key point box has been included to reinforce the information. This has been included for ease of reference for the reader.

Case Studies and Examples

Where these are appropriate, the material in the text will be related to case studies and examples to give an indication of how the issue relates to the practical business of police family liaison.

Chapter Summary

Each chapter concludes with a summary that draws together the key themes.

Space for Notes

Finally, each chapter includes a section at the end that allows space for practitioners to compile their own notes or information relating to points covered within the chapter.

1

Police Family Liaison

1.1 **Introduction**

There is no mystery to family liaison. It is simply the way in which the police as an organization communicates with some of its customers. What makes it warrant special attention is the position of the police as an organization and the expectations that are rightly placed on it by a well-informed society as well as the fact that the communication takes place at the very worst time of the customers' lives.

The relationship between the police and its customers is easily defined in the many roles that the police play. For instance, if a house is burgled, a car is stolen or someone assaulted, the police have a clear responsibility to communicate with the victim of the crime. They will often attend the victim's home and gather all possible information from them regarding the crime. They will be interested in how, when and where it occurred, as well as attempting to identify any forensic opportunities that might help to identify an offender. They will conduct local enquiries near the scene of the crime in a search for potential witnesses. They may even pass the victim's details on to another agency where they can receive additional support and arrange a follow up visit from a crime prevention officer. All these activities might be thought of as forms of victim or family liaison that are intended to enhance an investigation as well as reassure the public and prevent any further victimization. This tried and tested template for an investigation is what many people expect of the police where there is a 'victim of crime' or an 'injured party'.

The type of family liaison that this book is intended to describe is where the victim of the crime or incident is dead. The relationship is not between the police and the kind of victim who may be in a position to tell them exactly what happened; it is rather between the police and the bereaved relatives and friends of the victim.

The definition of 'family' for the purposes of police family liaison was described by the Association of Chief Police Officers (ACPO) in 2008 as follows:

- partners;
- parents;
- siblings;
- children;
- guardians;
- and others who have had a direct and close relationship with the victim.

The term 'family' thus includes 'chosen' family and should be reflective of the victim's culture and lifestyle. It is not simply an 'obligation' to next of kin, but a wider relationship designed to maximize knowledge of the victim or 'victimology' by speaking to those who know most about them. After all, with any other type of crime the police would usually have access to the victim themselves; when the victim of a crime is killed they have to reconstruct what is known about the deceased by talking to others.

The police also have an obligation to engage in a two-way information exchange that will hopefully keep the family updated on the progress of the investigation. If this is done effectively it should mitigate, as far as possible, any negative effects of the criminal justice system by the provision of timely accurate information to the family concerning coronial procedures as well as many of the other complexities that the family will encounter at this most tragic of times.

The relationship between the police and the communities that they serve is rarely more important than in times of crisis. Families and communities look to the lead agencies to respond appropriately. A solid professional partnership between family and police is to everybody's advantage. After all, the police have travelled down the same road many times before and have a fair idea of what is ahead. Most families have never been this way before; the very least they should have is a guide.

1.2 The Development of Police Family Liaison

The function of family liaison in homicide cases has been carried out for many years within the police service. The responsibility for making it happen sits with the officer in charge of the investigation. There does not seem to be any single significant event in the history of policing that inspired its introduction to investigation. It appears to have evolved almost as a moral or ethical responsibility that fell to the police as the lead agency.

In the past, however, family liaison bore little similarity to the service provided today. For many years the liaison function did not have a label and those performing it had no job description. It was merely the responsibility of the senior investigating officer (SIO) to communicate with the family at the early stages of the investigation. The purpose of this was to make sure that a formal identification of the victim was made and to reassure the family as to the commitment of the investigation team. In addition to this it also provided an opportunity to make an early attempt to establish a possible motive for the murder.

After initial contact from the SIO there was usually very little in the way of systematic liaison unless the investigation specifically required it or there was a significant piece of news to give out, whereupon the SIO or their deputy would return to speak with the relatives.

Much of this informal liaison relied on the individual and how comfortable he or she felt working with bereaved relatives. There were certainly no guidelines or any specific training for SIOs to refer to. It would be wrong, however, to assume that families never got a good service from the police because many

SIOs gave enormous amounts of energy to this task; anecdotal accounts suggest that in some high profile cases SIO and the family of the deceased stayed in touch for many years after the court case was finished.

The linked series of murders committed by Peter Sutcliffe in the 1970s had a significant impact on how the British police managed the large amounts of information and data in a major crime investigation. It also had a profound impact on the responsibilities of SIO. As the responsibilities of SIOs, the scope of their role and the things that the police service was accountable for all increased the management of major enquiries began to change. It was at about this time in the late 1970s and early 1980s that the role of 'family liaison officer' began to emerge. There was recognition that this was a role that needed more attention and that the SIO with all their other responsibilities may not be the most appropriate person to deliver it.

There is evidence to show that the role was being given some serious thought at this stage and there is no doubt that some excellent work was done by individuals performing the role. It was, however, still dependent on the qualities of the individual and the role would probably have been a little less demanding than it is today because families have a greater awareness of their right to ask about the progress of investigation.

Selection of staff for the role was ad hoc and the liaison task was often delegated to inexperienced officers who were thought to have more compassionate qualities. The history of the police service tends to show that at this time those roles were often reserved for women officers in a clear role demarcation and in the mistaken understanding that they could show the more caring side of policing while the men got on with the investigation. So it appears that unless there was a specific investigative reason, the role had started to develop into one where the police showed more compassion than investigative skills. It was some time before the police service recognized that the role demanded a fusion of compassion and investigative skills. As a consequence, during the 1980s and early 1990s few detectives volunteered to be the liaison between the investigation and the family when a homicide occurred. It was rather the case that the role during this time was usually performed by well-intentioned individuals with limited investigative skills who had to make it up as they went along.

1.3 Deployment

During the 1980s and early 1990s an officer would often be despatched to be with the family in the hours immediately after a homicide. The choice of officer was generally based on availability and sometimes, to avoid losing a detective from the overall investigation team, a uniformed officer from the local area would be seconded in.

At this particular time there were no dedicated homicide investigation teams in the UK; when a murder occurred a squad was formed from the detectives that were available locally. It seems reasonable to suggest that an ad hoc approach was sometimes taken when nominating a family liaison officer, in that matters progressed from a situation in which the SIO took personal responsibility for liaison with the family to a situation in which the nearest available member of the investigation team was delegated with the responsibility. While some such deployments worked remarkably well, others could have been better. It seemed then that the effectiveness of family liaison was a matter of chance.

There were no training courses for family liaison officers to go on to learn how to perform their role. The fact that it had often been performed by experienced detectives up until that point at least meant that the officers should, in principle, be able to explain the inner workings of a homicide investigation to the family. The introduction of less experienced detective and uniform officers into the liaison role, however, made for inconstant deliveries in the standard of service and some confusion as to what the role was really about. With the benefit of hindsight the issue is now clear: the ad hoc nature of family liaison officer deployment at the time was such that the police were often asking their less experienced officers to perform this most demanding of roles. With no proper selection criteria, no training and inconsistent levels of supervision and support, inexperienced staff were exposed to traumatized bereaved people and traumatized bereaved people were exposed to inexperienced staff.

On many occasions the police were working with people from minority ethnic communities and in some of those communities trust and confidence in policing was, at this time, very low. In almost all cases the police were liaising with people who had no conception of how the criminal justice system worked.

To add to this complexity, the culture within the police service was not to share information about an investigation. The balance on what to share and what not to share was, therefore, weighted against the family. This was not necessarily for malicious reasons; it was rather simply the way the police did business. There was also a misplaced idea that families did not want or need information and that the police were acting in the best interests of the family by keeping potentially distressing material away from them.

SIOs often made a decision to limit the amount of information regarding the progress of the investigation that they provided family liaison officers in the sincere belief that the provision of such information might compromise the officer in their role. This included not inviting them along to the regular briefings that the other members of the investigation team were having. The result of this was that they were not fully sighted on what was happening in the investigation. From the SIO's point of view withholding information about the progress of the investigation had an advantage in that it meant that the family liaison officer could not inadvertently release details to the family that might jeopardize the investigation. On the other hand, it had the effect of compromising the liaison function in that it meant that the family liaison officer could not provide the family with the kind of information that might reassure them that the death of their loved one was being properly investigated. It also meant that investigative opportunities arising from information supplied by the family may have been needlessly lost because they might not have been recognized as such by the family liaison officer.

The officers were often working for long periods of time in isolation, away from the rest of the investigation team. They had little to offer the family in the way of information about the investigation, they were operating with people who sometimes did not trust them anyway and, if they were inexperienced (as was often the case), they did not have the operational knowledge to explain what was going to happen next in terms of the workings of the criminal justice system. This all added up to making them extremely vulnerable as individuals, to the extent that family liaison officers often felt that they were performing a thankless task that no one else wanted to do and that their own colleagues did not understand or appreciate the difficulties involved.

1.4 **Recognition**

By the beginning of the 1990s some people who had performed the liaison role and understood its complexities were trying to do something to help others who were deployed as family liaison officers. Some training even began take place in a few places around the UK but this bottom-up process was due to the drive and determination of a few committed individuals and was by no means widespread.

The training that took place at this time was not to a common minimum standard. For the most part it amounted to a general awareness of the role so that officers being deployed for the first time would have some understanding of what family liaison was about. There was, however, a developing understanding of the important contribution that a family can make to the investigation as well as an acknowledgment that the police service was operating in a highly sensitive area without the appropriate resources.

Family liaison officers were also now being deployed into cases where a death on the road was being investigated; this role provided its own challenges for untrained staff, particularly given the fact that many more people die on the roads each year than die in homicides. The sheer volume of deaths that traffic investigators had to deal with added to the already challenging role. In addition to this, the criminal justice system can add to a family's trauma, given that sentences for causing a death on the road are considerably less than those associated with murder and manslaughter. Even where it was possible to secure a prosecution and a conviction, the sentences handed down for causing a death on the road were often seen by the families as being derisory. The pain of losing a loved one in a sudden and violent criminal act with a car was just as intense to a family and the family liaison officer was often in the front line when it came to soaking up the injustice felt by the relatives toward the criminal justice system.

Around this time there was also a developing recognition that the family liaison officer was being exposed to lengthy periods of emotionally draining work and that this could have an impact on their health.

Family liaison work was thus beginning to evolve. It was, however, very slow and disparate around the UK. The event that changed all of this, and the whole police approach when dealing with bereaved families, was the racist murder of Stephen Lawrence in 1993.

1.5 Stephen Lawrence

On 22 April 1993 a black teenager called Stephen Lawrence was stabbed to death by a group of white youths in Eltham, South London. To date no one has been convicted of Stephen's murder.

The weaknesses of the police investigation into Stephen's death were highlighted when on 24 March 1998 a public inquiry headed by Sir William Macpherson opened in South London. It is beyond the scope of this book to go over all the many issues raised about the investigation. The matters pertaining to the police family liaison were, however, pivotal in the development of the family liaison officers' role and it is to these matters that we shall now turn.

The report of the public inquiry into the death of Stephen Lawrence was finally released on 24 February 1999 and contained criticism of many agencies as well as the police service. The report went on to make recommendations about changes to the law and guidelines to drive race awareness education. At the very beginning of the recommendations were the words 'openness', 'accountability' and the restoration of 'confidence', and the first recommendation is that a ministerial priority be established for all police forces in England and Wales 'to increase trust and confidence in policing among minority ethnic communities'. This is a core principle in UK policing now; openness and accountability sit at the heart of family liaison work.

While reading the sections that follow it is important to remember that while it might be tempting to think that the criticism from the Stephen Lawrence Inquiry are a problem that was exclusive to the Metropolitan Police in London, its recommendations are directed to 'all police services' in England and Wales.

1.6 Family Liaison Recommendations

> 23. That Police Services should ensure that at local level there are readily available designated and trained Family Liaison Officers.

There are four components to this recommendation:

- Family liaison officers should be available at 'local level' because this would certainly assist at the earliest stage in an investigation by avoiding having the family left without assistance for a period of time until a suitable staff member is found from another area.

- 'Readily available' reinforces the early deployment criteria as well as underlining the importance of the role and the fact that line managers should ensure that appropriate staff are released without undue delay for such critical duties. Family liaison officers seldom have the authority to make *themselves* readily available, the onus of responsibility falls on those who manage them.
- 'Designated' implies that there should be an element of preparedness; the police should make the same provisions for the deployment of family liaison officers as they would for other specialist roles such as advanced police drivers or custody officers.
- The fourth point had clearly been identified by practitioners themselves before Stephen's death; 'training' was a fundamental issue. How could officers possibly be expected to perform in a specialist role with no training?

One of the jobs now was to look at what that training should look like as well as bringing together the most appropriate candidates for training.

> 24. That training of Family Liaison Officers must include training in racism awareness and cultural diversity, so that families are treated appropriately, professionally, with respect and according to their needs.

This was one recommendation that the police service actually took further; awareness training was rolled out to all police officers. It is a prerequisite to being selected for a family liaison course that candidates have successfully undergone community race relations training. In addition to this, some of the cultural issues associated with death are now covered in family liaison officer training, including some of the dilemmas that might face an investigation when trying to balance investigative needs against the cultural needs of a family.

> 25. That Family Liaison Officers shall, where appointed, be dedicated primarily if not exclusively to that task.

This recommendation is an acknowledgment of the importance of the role and that an officer should not be deployed as a family liaison officer on top of other core duties. The family need to know who their single point of contact is and when they are available; it is essential that family liaison officers and their managers understand this point.

> 26. That Senior Investigating Officers and Family Liaison Officers be made aware that good practice and their positive duty shall be the satisfactory management of family liaison, together with the provision to a victim's family all possible information about the crime and its investigation.

The introduction of the term 'satisfactory management' is important here as well as the fact the link is made back to the SIO.

While it is clear that the gap between the SIO and the family liaison officer has to be bridged to make sure that liaison is effectively delivered, the effect of this recommendation is to emphasize the need for the organization to take some responsibility for effective liaison as well as the individuals who work for it.

The point about 'provision of all possible information about the crime and its investigation' in recommendation 26 is, perhaps, the one that required the biggest change in the approach traditionally taken by the police up until that time. It went to the very heart of police culture at the time. Police officers can be fiercely protective of their investigations, often for the best possible reasons. No police officer wanted to see a solid case lost because a piece of information had inappropriately slipped into the public domain.

It is, however, easy to forget that families tend to share this point of view; they do not want to see the case lost either. The issue then is not about the release of 'all information' but about the release of 'all *possible* information'. It is sometimes not appropriate to release all the information during an investigation for a variety of reasons. Certain information could compromise a line of enquiry or even put someone's life at risk. So this recommendation did not remove the decision-making power as to what information to release from the SIO; indeed it emphasized the importance of exercising good judgment and made it clear that the police should respect families enough to explain the issues to them. It is, for example, legitimate to tell a family that 'there are certain issues that we cannot discuss with you at this moment and the reasons for that are …' and '… as soon as we can release this information to you we will'. The justified withholding of information cannot be open ended; giving the family some idea of when the information can be shared with them is a matter of good practice.

> 27. That good practice shall provide that any request made by the family of a victim which is not acceded to, and any complaint by any member of the family, shall be formally recorded by the SIO and shall be reported to the immediate superior officer.

There are clear references here to the fact that the Lawrence family had on a number of occasions expressed their dissatisfaction about the way that they were being dealt with. That there were few records of these concerns added to the family's irritation with the investigation and made the police look unprofessional. This links back to the previous recommendation in that it makes it clear that a family has rights and that should the police (or any other agency for that matter) be unable to meet any request that they make to exercise those rights a record should be made and an explanation given. Should the family be dissatisfied with such an explanation it should also be recorded and brought to the attention of a senior manager as soon as possible.

As a consequence of this recommendation, family liaison logs were designed and introduced; they are the family liaison officer's record of meetings with the family and should be supervised by the SIO on a regular basis.

> 28. That police services and Victim Support Services ensure that their systems provide for the proactive use of local contacts within minority ethnic communities to assist with family liaison where appropriate.

This was a reference to the need to develop better community relationships when dealing with the aftermath of personal tragedy. The issue here was that it was often the practice of the police to only rely on other statutory agencies. The public inquiry into Stephen's death highlighted major failings that prevented many fine community groups and advocates from being given the opportunity to make a valuable contribution toward liaison between the police and the family. It emphasized the need to reach out to 'hard-to-hear' communities and to take a more holistic approach to policing. This further endorsed the need to build trust and confidence within minority ethnic communities.

1.7 The Post-Lawrence Policing Environment

The aftermath of the Stephen Lawrence Inquiry saw the most widespread and sweeping changes in policing for many years. From a family liaison perspective the Metropolitan Police Service were under immense pressure to make progress in implementing these recommendations.

Fortunately the Metropolitan Police Service had been watching the public inquiry very closely and had recognized long before the report was published that family liaison was a major issue that needed to be addressed. So from the beginning of 1999 a dedicated family liaison team was set up in London to take the issue forward. This team sat under the leadership of Deputy Assistant Commissioner John Grieve and was given the remit by him to do whatever had to be done to get this piece of business on track.

The first thing that needed to be developed was a training course that would equip the staff for the role. There were, however, no books available for this type of work. It was a role that was fairly unique to the police. Other emergency services came into contact with relatives when someone was killed but the police role was firmly rooted in investigation and took in a range of responsibilities. As well as establishing the identity of the deceased the police were charged with finding out how they died and who was responsible for their death. Then, if they were going to be able to deliver any form of justice to the family, they had to secure a safe conviction at court.

The Metropolitan Police Service looked around for help in this area and developed a significant partnership with Avon and Somerset Constabulary. They had been closely watching events during the public inquiry as well and had acted by designing and running the first family liaison course in the UK that really reflected the Stephen Lawrence recommendations. This relationship proved beneficial to both forces and over the next eighteen months substantial learning and development took place across the field of police family liaison.

Many other forces tapped in to the training being offered by Avon and Somerset and important relationships were formed nationally that benefited the development of good practice in family liaison. Many of those relationships endure to this day. This proved to be of considerable benefit because there were some significant incidents for the police to respond to. The amount of homicides and road deaths that occur in the UK did not diminish as the police came under ever increasing scrutiny at this time. How the police investigated a suspicious death was being examined in the media and the reporting was rarely complimentary.

1.8 The Nail Bombings

In April 1999 a thirteen-day nail bombing campaign took place in London. The first attack took place on Saturday 17 April in a crowded street in Brixton. The street at this time was busy with weekend shoppers. Fifty people were injured, many of them seriously, and it was remarkable that no one was actually killed. Brixton, where the 1981 riots took place has a predominantly black community and the police considered the possibility that this was a racially motivated crime from the earliest stage of the investigation.

The police were definitely under pressure to respond appropriately to the concerns of the local community, as well as make an early arrest. Many of the relationships forged with the local community after the Stephen Lawrence Report proved crucial. Police and community were working together in an effort to solve this crime and create an environment of mutual trust.

The suspect was still at large by the following Saturday, 24 April, when another bomb went off, this time near Brick Lane in the East End of London, a predominantly Bengali area. Thirteen people were injured on this occasion. Again, positive relationships between the police and the local community helped greatly. There was, however, tremendous media interest and a building concern within all of London's communities as to who was next and where the next bomb was going to go off.

The third and last bomb exploded on Friday 30 April, this time inside a crowded pub in the heart of London. The 'Admiral Duncan' public house was a well-known meeting place for the lesbian and gay community, but was also frequented by people finishing work for the night and by theatre goers. On an early Friday evening it was very busy inside.

Three people were killed and seventy nine people injured; four of them required amputations. The Metropolitan Police Service deployed several of their newly trained family liaison officers and successfully reached out for assistance into another minority community.

The deployment of these newly trained family liaison officers turned out to be crucial both for the investigation and for the families. It was a difficult time for all concerned. At this time, however, the Metropolitan Police Service had only around fifteen fully trained family liaison officers. The service was so worried that the bomber would cause mass fatalities that on the day of the last bombing they had given around a hundred officers a family liaison awareness training course. The course was only one day and was not intended to replace the full authorized family liaison officers' course. It was, however, an emergency and it was thought that the resilience provided by the availability of additional resources was needed in this area. Many of the one-day awareness trained officers found themselves being called out before they had even arrived back home on 30 April.

David Copeland was arrested for the bombings late in the evening of 30 April after a tip-off. The tip-off was triggered by the release of CCTV images to the media by police from the Anti Terrorist Branch and a wider terror campaign against London's minority communities was thus avoided. The nail bombings, however, served as a chilling reminder to the Metropolitan Police Service of the devastating impact of terror and the implications of a potential mass fatality incident, not only on police operations in general but on family liaison resources.

1.9 **Marchioness Disaster**

The Marchioness disaster was another significant event in the development of family liaison as we know it today, although it probably was not recognized as such at the time.

By April 1999 when the nail bombings happened there was no written policy or strategy for family liaison in London or anywhere else. There was a general understanding at this stage that family liaison officers would be deployed into homicides everywhere and deaths on the road in some but not all areas.

The nail bombings had served as a timely reminder that a mass fatality terrorist incident could take place in the UK and that the police would struggle to cope with the family liaison implications if it did. The nail bombs were, however, a very clear criminal act, a mass homicide. There was no police position on a mass fatality incident that was less clear on cause or blame, or even one where the police did not have primacy over the investigation.

On 20 August 1989 a disaster occurred on the River Thames in London. A dredger known as 'The Bowbelle' collided with a pleasure craft called 'The Marchioness'. Fifty one young people died in the incident and a massive investigation was launched by the Marine Accident Investigation Branch. The Metropolitan Police Service, however, had the responsibility for managing the recovery of bodies, mortuary arrangements and the identification process.

On 7 April 1995 a coroner's inquest ordered that the victims had been unlawfully killed and a public inquiry was launched on 2 October 2000, chaired by Lord Justice Clarke.

While this incident had actually taken place before the death of Stephen Lawrence the public inquiry into it took place over two years after the one into the death of Stephen. Having been through the Stephen Lawrence Inquiry, the Metropolitan Police Service was now much more aware of the type of examination that the organization was going to be put through. An in-depth review of systems for managing mass fatality incidents was being prepared in the build-up to the inquiry and one of the things that was looked at was the potential for using family liaison officers in the aftermath of a mass fatality to gather and obtain ante mortem information from the bereaved relatives. This was in keeping with the contribution made to the investigation by the Metropolitan Police Service.

Discussions took place between the police team preparing for the public inquiry and the Family Liaison Team for the Metropolitan Police Service and an agreement was made in principal that in the event of a major disaster where there was large-scale loss of life family liaison officers could be used, if required by the person leading that part of the investigation, to collect the data from the families as well as acting as a conduit for information between the family and the investigation.

This was an agreement in principal and would later be endorsed by Lord Justice Clarke in the Marchioness public inquiry. In the time between 'agreement in principle' and the publication of the inquiry's recommendations, however, the Ladbroke Grove rail crash took place and the Metropolitan Police Service made a decision to deploy family liaison officers to a major disaster incident involving mass fatalities for the first time.

On 5 October 1999 thirty one people died at Ladbroke Grove and 227 were hospitalized. A further 296 were treated at the site for minor injuries. Given that the crash took place shortly after the nail bombs, family liaison resources were stretched with this further deployment. A total of 111 family liaison officers were deployed within forty eight hours of the crash. These were made up of a mixture of staff that had been on the authorized course and staff who had the one-day awareness training on the day of the 'Admiral Duncan' public house nail bombing.

The family liaison deployments were later seen by police and families as having been beneficial but it had introduced staff into a new arena and training had to be developed to accommodate this. The fact that the police had effectively tested their family liaison response in real circumstances probably confirmed to Lord Justice Clarke the importance of this type of work by the lead agencies in the disaster, because in his report into the Marchioness he later stated the following:

> Family Liaison will be a major part of the police response to a disaster, particularly in the identification process ... These officers will have a crucial role to play in the identification process, which extends beyond that for a normal homicide investigation.
>
> The Family liaison officer has a key role, both in the identification and investigation process.

He then went on to lay out some general principles for identification processes after disasters:

- *Provision of honest and, as far as possible, accurate information at all times and at every stage.* This was very similar to what had come out of the Stephen

Lawrence inquiry and was also based on the right of families to know. This was very significant and served to further emphasize the needs of the victim and their family.

- *Respect for the deceased and the bereaved.* Respect for the deceased and the bereaved relates to all disciplines and organizations responding to this type of incident, the first person who takes a missing person report on the telephone, the extraordinary people who recover human remains from disaster sites, the mortuary staff and the family liaison officers. It also seems likely that it was meant to include all levels of staff responding in each respective agency; as with the Stephen Lawrence inquiry, criticism was not solely aimed at the police by Lord Justice Clarke.
- *A sympathetic and caring approach throughout.* This principle is another acknowledgment of what the families were going through at the very worst time of their lives and the need for practitioners to have that at the forefront of their minds throughout the investigation.
- *The avoidance of mistaken identity.* This principle emphasizes the importance of a high level of professionalism that needs to be evident in the aftermath of this type of event.

In mass disaster the identification process, which is dictated in England, Wales and Northern Ireland by an Identification Commission chaired by the coroner (the Procurator Fiscal in Scotland), is likely to be forensic rather than visual due to the potential for mistaken identification where there is disruption to bodies. Forensic collection by family liaison officers or other practitioners must be able to stand up to the highest standards of scrutiny. The same applies to the work being conducted at the mortuary.

Family liaison had now moved a considerable distance in a very short space of time and it was time to take stock and make some proper plans.

1.10 **Family Liaison Guidelines**

Following the Ladbroke Grove disaster a debrief was held and many lessons were learnt from the family liaison officers involved about the issues that they faced when dealing with this type of incident. One thing that clearly shone through was the need for guidelines or operating protocols.

Even though an extensive training programme was now under way in London to give the Metropolitan Police Service the capacity to resource large deployments if necessary, more needed to be done. Since the new family liaison officers had received very little training in respect of their role in mass fatality investigations there was still an element of staff having to 'make it up as they went along'. By and large the training had equipped them for a homicide or a roads policing deployment involving a single fatality but the complexities of a mass fatality incident were new to everyone.

The need for proper coordination and leadership was also emphasized in the Ladbroke Grove debriefing. Much of the effort in the years that preceded Ladbroke Grove had been in getting enough family liaison officers trained. What had happened at Ladbroke Grove showed that many of the other members of the organization still considered their work a bit of a mystery. It was clear that a coordination function had to be introduced: a role for managers who understood what the family liaison officers do, a role for someone to create an environment for them to succeed.

The Metropolitan Police ran the first family liaison coordinators course in March of 2001. The Metropolitan Police Family Liaison Team set about developing guidelines for London, which were released on 29 March 2001. They were entitled the *Metropolitan Police Family Liaison Principles and Fundamental Guidelines*.

1.11 **11 September 2001**

The development of written family liaison guidelines was instrumental in how the British police responded to the terrorist attacks on the World Trade Center and the Pentagon on 11 September 2001. There was, however, no precedent for 9/11. While Ladbroke Grove had been the first time trained family liaison officers had been deployed into a major disaster in the UK, 9/11 became the first time they had been deployed in a disaster investigation in another country or for that matter another continent.

In the hours after the World Trade Center attacks it was known that some level of police family liaison was going to be necessary. The Metropolitan Police Casualty Bureau had been opened and reports of missing British citizens were starting to come in. A sizeable minority of the people in the World Trade Center on 11 September had been British. Some worked there, some were attending a conference and some were visiting for other reasons.

Many British relatives had watched the events unfold on live television, not knowing whether their loved one had survived or not. Many of these relatives were making their way to the US, then finding a way of getting into New York to search for information about their loved ones. This had not been anticipated because the airspace around New York was closed; but families flew to Florida or Canada and hired cars or caught trains in a desperate attempt to find out more information.

The British Consulate in New York was soon overwhelmed with British families, and even if they had had the staff to deal with them there was a limit to what they could offer them in New York at this time. There was a massive disaster response going on and good quality communication between local, regional, national and international agencies was still being developed.

The Foreign and Commonwealth Office had picked up some of the positive media around family liaison officers following Ladbroke Grove and they made an approach to the Metropolitan Police Service on 15 September asking for twenty family liaison officers to go to New York to assist them with the British families. This was agreed to, and a Metropolitan Police led team made up of family liaison officers from around the UK was despatched to New York. While they had very little in the way of a plan, they were in possession of some very precious resources: trained staff, working guidelines and family liaison logs and this all contributed to a very successful deployment.

1.12 Learning the Lessons

The history of family liaison has up to now been shaped by events. Many of these events have been outside the control of anyone. What is important though is that lessons continue to be learnt. A modern organization should never be guilty of making the same mistakes over and over again. This chapter has reported on some of the events that shaped the early development of family liaison in the police service. Many mistakes have been made along the way but they have been learnt from and turned into training opportunities.

The events described in this chapter were novel environments for family liaison officers. There have been many more since; for example the Bali bombings in Indonesia and the Asian Tsunami were events that were beyond anything that conventional police planning could ever have predicted. The London bombs of 7 July 2005 introduced the new concept in the UK of the family assistance centre, which was another new environment for family liaison practitioners. There have been more domestic train crashes, in Selby, Hatfield, Ufton Nervet and Potters Bar and tragically there were fatalities in all them. There was the tragedy in Morecombe Bay when at least twenty one Chinese nationals drowned, bringing complexities in identification as well as investigation. There have also been many high profile homicide investigations like Soham and the linked murders of five young women in Ipswich, countless low profile but highly complex homicide investigations and thousands of road deaths where family liaison officers and family liaison coordinators have done some extraordinary work.

There is also a lot of resource material that we can learn from. For example, we can look back safely at events that happened before family liaison—events such as Lockerbie, Dunblane, Hungerford, Zeebrugge, Hillsborough and as far back as Aberfan—and think about how we might approach them in today's policing environment. There are lessons still to be learned.

Every police service in the UK now has trained family liaison officers as well as dedicated family liaison coordinators. The Association of Chief Police Officers published the first national *Family Liaison Strategy Manual* in 2003; the document was revised and re-emerged as the *Family liaison officer Guidance* in 2008. The training of family liaison officers continues to develop to meet the ever-changing environment. There are regional and national forums for the exchange of good practice to ensure development through learning.

The history and the mistakes should never be forgotten though and there is always a temptation to think that what has been achieved is some sort of finished article. It is far from it; complacency is one of the biggest dangers facing the discipline. This book is intended to stimulate a discussion that encourages police officers and partner agencies to consider the nature of family liaison and the challenges that face it.

The book is not just for practitioners. Delivery of family liaison is the overarching responsibility of the organization as a whole, from the top to the bottom. It is how we communicate with our customers in the most traumatic circumstances. It follows that no family liaison function can be truly successful unless it is resourced, supervised and supported throughout the organization.

When families allow the police into their home in the aftermath of a tragedy they are entitled to the most effective, professional and compassionate investigation that can possibly be achieved. That is why we need to use the best and most appropriate staff; we need to select the right people, give them the right training and deploy them with an effective strategy along with the best possible support and supervision.

Families do not ask the police for friendship or care, but for an effective, inclusive investigation that allows justice to take its course. History will judge the police harshly, if after two public inquiries, the investigative function served by family liaison is mistaken for something akin to a social service. After all, the parents of Stephen Lawrence wanted the one thing that the police did not deliver—the safe and successful conviction of the people who had murdered Stephen.

NOTES

NOTES

2

Organizational Support for Family Liaison

2.1 **Introduction**

Family liaison officers cannot succeed unless they are supported by an organizational framework. Figure 1 is intended to illustrate such a framework. While such a framework is fundamental to ensure local, regional and national excellence, a solid working philosophy is essential to make it work. This chapter sets out to consider the organizational framework that is required to support police family liaison and the philosophy that is needed to underpin it.

2.2 **Organizational Philosophy**

There is more to learning lessons than just setting an agenda for change; at some point the leaders of an organization have to take the staff with them and inspire them to succeed. This section focuses on the organizational philosophy that is necessary for the leaders of an organization to promote family liaison. While it was written around the role of family liaison it could equally apply to other roles within a modern organization.

The kind of organizational philosophy that underpins successful family liaison is, perhaps, best considered in terms of:

- the statement of principle that encapsulates it; and
- its scope.

Figure 2.1 Family liaison framework McGarry D. (2004) 'Organizational Structure for effective Family Liaison', a presentation to the Family Assistance Foundation Symposium, in Atlanta USA

2.2.1 A Statement of principle

The statement of principle that encapsulates an organizational philosophy for family liaison is:

> In the event of a death of a human being,
> Where there is a police investigation,
> The police have a positive duty,
> To communicate effectively and inclusively,
> With the bereaved family and friends.

This does not prevent family liaison officers from being deployed in cases that fall outside this definition provided those responsible for their welfare and supervision are mindful that they should not venture into situations that they are not trained to deal with or into areas where another staff member would be more appropriate. It is also important to recognize circumstances where there is a need for additional resources and supervision.

The working assumption encapsulating the organizational philosophy for family liaison can, perhaps, be best considered by breaking it down into its component parts:

1) *'In the event of the death of a human being where there is a police investigation'* might sound self-explanatory but the police deal with a variety of situations in which death occurs and there is not always an investigation. It can, for example, be very tempting to deploy a family liaison officer when someone dies tragically through a sudden illness, but it should always be remembered that the family liaison officer is an investigator and that where no police investigation is taking place the deployment of a family liaison officer will be of no strategic value to the organization or the family.

   A philosophy of engagement is important when deciding whether it is appropriate to deploy a family liaison officer. On many occasions since the publication of the Stephen Lawrence Inquiry Report (Home Office, 1999) and the Marchioness/Bowbelle Inquiry Report (Department for the Environment, Transport and the Regions, 2001) the deployment of a family liaison officer has been seen as the remedy for *any* problem relating to a family and/or a community. This kind of thinking is flawed because the solution may be engagement of staff with different skills and expertise. That many family liaison officers have become adept at dealing with a diverse range of critical incidents is testament to their training and experience. The need for their deployment should, however, always be risk assessed to ensure that they are really the most appropriate resource for the job in question. For example, in a kidnap situation a family liaison officer may present great communication skills with the family but be less adept at understanding and explaining the intricate workings of hostage negotiation.

   There may also be cases where an investigation into someone's death is taking place but is being led by a different investigative body, such as the

Health and Safety Executive. An example of this could be where someone has been killed in a fairground accident. In these circumstances the agency that should be communicating with the relatives is the one leading the investigation. This is, however, an area where developments are taking place and it is possible that with new legislation in England and Wales that relates to corporate manslaughter a family liaison officer may indeed end up being the most appropriate deployment.

2) *'The police have a positive duty'*. This part of the statement of principle is intended to mainstream family liaison into modern policing. It is not a reward for 'nice' victims, it is not reserved for more complex cases, and it is not something forced upon the police due to previous mistakes: it is the positive duty of the police to provide this service whenever there is a police investigation into the death of a human being.
3) *'Communicate effectively and inclusively'*. Effective communication is a two-way process. The family needs to know and understand what is happening and the police need to know and understand as much as possible about the victim, their lifestyle and victimology. If both sides of this communication are right the family's interaction with the criminal justice system will be effective.
4) *'Inclusively'* is intended to embrace and emphasize the partnership approach taken to modern policing by sharing all possible information with the family. This has very positive investigative benefits. The sharing of information should not be looked upon as a reward but as a means to unlocking key information that may help to explain why someone has been killed.
5) *'With the bereaved family and friends'*. The first national Family Liaison Strategy (Association of Chief Police Officers for England and Wales, 2003) stated that the term family should include:

   - partners;
   - parents;
   - siblings;
   - children;
   - guardians; and
   - others who have had a direct and close relationship with the victim.

The purpose for this wide definition is to allow for the fact that the word 'family' may have different meanings between different cultures and nationalities. It is also intended to provide for gay and lesbian couples who are not in a formal partnership to be treated equally in the eyes of the investigation.

This definition acknowledges that the police service has obligations that are not confined solely to next of kin. There are great investigative advantages to such a broad approach because it can enhance the picture that is developed of the victim and the environment around them. The police response to the next of kin of a deceased person should not be undermined by this approach, but it may be important to consider the deployment of additional family liaison staff, especially in the crucial early stages of an investigation.

2.2.2 **Scope**

To be successful a family liaison philosophy should cover:

- everybody within the organization, from the top to the bottom; and
- the relationship between the organization and external agencies and organizations that could support family liaison.

It is important that every member of staff understands that police family liaison is the responsibility of the organization and not just the individuals that perform the role. A wider understanding of the complexities of the role and the support of the whole of the police service to deliver it is important to its success. The principles of liaison should be at the heart of policing, and education about its importance should permeate the training of all staff. This includes first responders at the scene of a road death through to chief constables, those in charge of budgets through to front desk staff at a police station, scenes of crime staff through to those who recover human remains at the scene of a mass disaster. In the eyes of the community they are all 'the police' and as such contact should be professional, helpful, and effective.

Working with other appropriate agencies can also enhance the experience of families coming into contact with the criminal justice system. Part of the police response should, therefore, be the capability of either linking a family with another agency that can assist them or being able to 'signpost' them as to where they might find such assistance. It can be anything that may enhance communication with the family, such as interpreters or intermediaries, but it can also mean asking for help from various external partner agencies and organizations who may have expertise in areas such as culture and bereavement. It would be unwise for the police to 'branch out' into an area where training has not been provided. Family liaison officers and their supervisors should seek in advance to develop relationships and partnerships that are likely to assist an investigation. This can only enhance the way the police operate and cooperate within communities.

2.3 **National Operating Protocols**

It is important that family liaison is underpinned by some kind of doctrine or guidance. Such a doctrine should describe good practice. Good practice should be developed and promoted nationally. Every effort should be made to avoid a situation in which the quality of service provided by family liaison depends on where people live or where a death occurs.

In England and Wales each of the forty three different police forces has its own operational protocols. Family liaison is one of the disciplines in police work that is not limited by geographical boundaries. It covers a variety of situations where a death has occurred including homicide, road death, mass fatality and critical incidents. It is, therefore, essential that a national framework is established that supports the development of good family liaison. Within this framework practitioners of different disciplines and members of different police services can identify how to work together effectively and in partnership with other agencies.

The publication of the first *National Family Liaison Strategy* guidance in England and Wales in 2003 by the Association of Chief Police Officers was significant for a number of reasons:

- It provided key strategic stakeholder endorsement for the development of family liaison in the organization.
- It defined good practice and, thus, underpinned the training of everybody involved in family liaison.
- It ensured a consistent national standard of service between police forces.
- It described how family liaison linked in to other key investigative services within the organization.
- It described how police family liaison worked with partnership organizations to deliver an effective service.

A revised version of this document, entitled *Family Liaison Officer Guidance*, took account of the developments in family liaison that happened in response to the unique and often unplanned for events that the police service was confronted with in the intervening years between 2003 and 2008.

The existence of national guidance has increased the understanding across forces of the need for a corporate approach. It has also given people the direction that they need on occasion when dealing with a complex issue. The guidance is drawn from the history of family liaison and is testament to lessons learnt. It is, however, important to remember that new lessons are being learnt every day and a circulation of good practice is necessary for development. As a result, in the UK, national and regional user groups meet on a regular basis and a national conference takes place every year.

National guidance and developments in practice must be managed and supported. In the UK, this is achieved by means of a national structure involving the Association of Chief Police Officers. The appointment of a National Family Liaison Advisor lends added support to the national structure. The National Family Liaison Advisor is a police detective who has been seconded to the Crime Operational Support branch of the National Policing Improvement Agency. The National Family Liaison Advisor's role is to support and provide advice on current investigations as well as assist with training and policy development across all forces in the UK.

2.4 Training

Training of family liaison officers has always been the basis of successful practice. A national training programme for family liaison was implemented in the UK in 2008. The purpose of the programme is to professionalize and standardize training across all the forces of England, Wales and Northern Ireland. Before then, the training has been good, but perhaps a little varied across the policing community.

The increase in cross-border co-operation between forces had raised the need for national standards in training. The benefits of this training programme are that all family liaison officers are trained to the same high standard and can work successfully with colleagues from other forces using the same administration and investigation procedures. This was a very important step forward as some of the problems that emerged from mass fatality deployments were due to the variations in practice that were evident around the country. At worst these occasionally led to mixed messages being passed on to families and sometimes duplication of efforts and requests.

2.4.1 Selection criteria for training

The role of family liaison officer is not suited to all staff, and managers need to develop and apply appropriate criteria when selecting people to be trained. Such selection criteria need to focus on two areas:

1) the availability to perform the role of family liaison officer; and
2) the suitability of the individual for the role.

The availability of the person for the role simply refers to them being in a role where deployment as a family liaison officer is a realistic possibility. There is no point in training a person to be a family liaison officer if they are in another role that is likely to exclude them from operational practice in family liaison, such as might be the case with officers in another specialist role. For example, an officer who has been trained in and irregularly deployed in covert operational activity may be unlikely to ever be available for deployment as a family liaison officer as a result of their other duties.

The suitability of the individual for the role refers to their personal qualities rather than their position. To be eligible for training as a family liaison officer people should be:

- good at communicating with and listening to other people;
- confident;
- able to work under pressure; and
- able to work independently.

2.4.2 **The training**

The national training is a minimum standard and it still allows for forces to add additional material for their students that reflects local policing issues. It is important to stress that the training course in itself is just part of a programme. The professional family liaison officer should have additional training within their force at least once a year. Their performance in the role should also be monitored by a supervisor and they will need to provide evidence to show that they continue to reach the standards required.

The general areas covered in the training should include:

- the role of the family liaison officer and the system governing their deployment in the force concerned;
- family liaison strategies;
- risk assessment;
- the impact of bereavement as a result of homicide on a family (including some of the social and cultural factors that affect grieving);
- the role of the coroner;
- the identification and classification of witnesses;
- victimology;
- the impact of media reporting on the family, the investigation and legal proceedings;
- record keeping;
- exit strategies;
- disaster victim identification;
- deaths abroad; and
- occupational health and welfare.

Family liaison officer training in England and Wales is governed by the *Family Liaison Officer Development Programme* (ACPO and the National Policing Improvement Agency, 2008). Further details of the training and a recommended course timetable are to be found in the *Development Programme*.

2.4.3 **Post-training course workplace mentoring and assessment**

It is important to understand that a training course can only provide the foundations of a competent performance in the workplace. While training is undoubtedly a necessary basis for good practice it is not and can never be a sufficient condition by itself for the delivery of a competent performance. As with any other skill, it needs to be carefully nurtured through the support of a mentor in the form of an experienced practitioner of the craft and set in the context of a developmental workplace-assessment regime.

2.5 **Support**

There is always a need for line managers and supervisors to play an active part in the family liaison function. It follows that training works best if paired with supervision and support.

It is essential that family liaison officers and supervisors are part of an occupational health scheme. How forces roll this out locally will be a matter for their own working practices, but the *Family Liaison Officer Guidance* (ACPO, 2008) makes this a prerequisite to continuing in the role. Support can range from informal meetings, debriefs, formal tasking, training days through to welfare meetings and, if necessary, taking the family liaison officer out of the role for a period of time.

Deployment of a staff member who is unsuitable for whatever reason presents an unacceptable risk to the individual themselves, the family they are working with and ultimately the reputation of the police service.

2.6 **Selection Criteria for Deployment**

Selection criteria should be applied before the selection of an individual for a particular deployment. Once trained it is important that each individual deployment is looked at and risk assessed according to the circumstances. Any weaknesses in these areas could undermine the family liaison strategy and result in ineffective investigation.

When any deployment is considered it is always important to take account of any factors in the family liaison officer's past or present circumstances that may give rise to a problem. Such problems could be either emotional (for example, having recently experienced a bereavement) or practical (for example, soon being on leave for an extensive period or being unavailable as a result of other work commitments such as a pending court case).

The continued deployment of a family liaison officer in an ongoing investigation should also be kept under constant review because circumstances may arise that might make it necessary to replace them with either a new family liaison officer or to provide another means of contact between the investigation team and the family. Such situations may arise, for example, where communication breaks down irrevocably between the family liaison officer and the family, where an unanticipated commitment arises, such as the family liaison officer being summonsed to court, or where something unexpectedly changes in the officer's domestic situation.

The family liaison officer has a responsibility to inform the SIO or the senior identification manager (SIM) of any issues that might make them unsuitable either for a new deployment or for continued deployment in an ongoing case.

KEY POINT – DEPLOYING FAMILY LIAISON OFFICERS

It is important to consider the following issues when deploying family liaison officers:

- risk assessment;
- prospective family liaison officer's current emotional suitability;
- any domestic or professional commitments that are likely to have an impact on the prospective family liaison officer's availability.

2.7 Supervision, Advice and Resources

Family liaison officers will often by necessity spend long periods of time working away from the rest of the investigation team. Supervisors should maintain contact with the family liaison officers throughout. The information that needs to pass both ways between police and family can change very quickly at critical stages of an investigation and family liaison officers will need to be able to get advice at very short notice.

The family liaison officer should never be allowed to feel isolated as this will potentially impact on their performance and the relationship with the family. The family liaison officer can often be seen by the family as the face of the police service. Family liaison officers can often feel the pressure that this responsibility brings.

In order to avoid this situation the family liaison officer should as far as possible attend all briefings and meetings. If for some operational reason this is not possible the supervisor(s) must arrange additional individual briefings for the family liaison officers. Records should be kept of all such briefings in accordance with the overall investigative strategy.

During the deployment it is highly likely that the family liaison officers will be required to work long hours and additional resources may be required to meet the needs of the family and the investigation. As previously mentioned, other agencies may be required to assist the relatives in areas that fall outside the police role. Nonetheless the family liaison officer will need access to someone with the authority to release resources in order that they can successfully perform their role.

There may be occasions where reference has to be drawn back to the working philosophy. The *'positive duty to communicate effectively and inclusively'* rests with the whole police service. The family liaison officer needs all the factors in this model to be in place and working to be successful now and in the longer term.

2.8 Chapter Summary

This chapter has suggested that family liaison officers can never work in isolation from the operational context in which they function. Such a context needs to be set within a framework underpinned by an appropriate organizational philosophy. Given that family liaison is not constrained by local boundaries and that it cuts across a variety of situations in which the investigation of a death might occur, such an organizational philosophy must be embodied in national guidance. The organizational philosophy drives the selection, training and deployment of family liaison officers.

NOTES

NOTES

3

Initial Contact with the Family

3.1 Introduction

It is essential to manage initial contact with the family well because it can exert a considerable influence over the pattern of interaction that follows. It can influence the disposition of the family toward the investigation, something that can be an important factor in ensuring their willingness to supply information and cooperate with its investigative strategies (ie media strategy). It can exert an influence on the extent to which the family are satisfied with the investigation. Making the purpose of family liaison clear from the outset can also help with the implementation of an exit strategy.

Before the initial contact takes place, however, a number of factors are likely to exert an influence on the quality of the interaction that is to take place between the family and the family liaison officer:

- early contact between the family and the police in respect of the incident that resulted in the death of the family member (eg when the family member was reported missing, when a local officer knocked on their door to inform them of the death);
- the SIO or SIM's family liaison strategy;
- the family's composition and history;
- the nature of the incident that led to the death of the family member.

All these factors are likely to have an impact on the way the police investigation is perceived and on the reception that is given to the family liaison officer by the family.

The starting point for this book is the role of family liaison. It is, therefore, beyond its scope to cover the myriad of situations in which early contact can take place between the family and the police in respect of the incident. The focus of this chapter is, however, very much on the development of a family liaison strategy by the senior investigating officer or senior identification manager and on the development of family liaison plans governing initial contact by the family liaison officer. The development of family liaison strategies and plans must always take account of the family's composition and history, and the nature of the incident that led to the death of the family member.

3.2 Family Liaison Strategies

In the UK the officer in charge of an investigation into a major crime (eg murder) or a road death is known as the senior investigating officer (SIO). In such cases the SIO is responsible for developing a family liaison strategy. Where mass fatalities have occurred as a result of a disaster, however, a senior identification manager (SIM) is likely to be appointed. As the title suggests, a SIM is responsible for ensuring that the victims of a disaster are properly identified. In disasters involving mass fatalities where a SIM has been appointed, the SIM is responsible for developing the family liaison strategy.

There can often be a great deal of confusion about what a strategy is and what a plan is to the extent that the terms are often used interchangeably. For the sake of clarity, this chapter considers a strategy to be a high level overview that governs the direction of family liaison in the context of the wider investigation, whereas a plan focuses on the tactical considerations involved in communicating with the family on a day-to-day basis. While they are separate entities in their own right, effective plans depend on good strategies. As noted, responsibility for developing and implementing the strategy falls to the SIO or the SIM, whereas responsibility for planning the details of contact with the family is a matter for the family liaison officer.

In the context of an investigation, strategies provide the basis for the overall direction and governance of any given group of techniques used in the enquiry. A major investigation, for example, is likely to include a forensic strategy, a media strategy, a house-to-house enquiry strategy and an interview strategy. These strategies do not stand in isolation from each other; a good strategy will always take account of any other that could have an impact on its business.

KEY POINT – STRATEGIES THAT COULD FEATURE IN A MAJOR INVESTIGATION

Depending on the circumstances of the case, the overarching investigation strategy for a major crime enquiry could include the following strategies:

- house-to-house enquiries;
- forensic;
- search;
- passive data generator (eg CCTV cameras);
- family liaison;
- media;
- internal communications (communication within the police service);
- interview (witness and suspect);
- elimination (elimination of individuals as potential suspects in the investigation);
- identification;
- covert enquiries.

Many major investigations, including road death and mass disaster as well as crime, can also benefit from a family liaison strategy. As with any other strategy, the SIO or SIM is responsible for the development and the implementation of the family liaison strategy. Strategies are dynamic and need to change as circumstances change. An initial strategy should be developed within the first few hours of the enquiry, usually before the family are visited, because it is an essential consideration when selecting and briefing a family liaison officer.

Example – relationships between the strategies in a major investigation

Family liaison strategies in major crime investigations are most likely to have a relationship with the media and interview strategies. In some cases there might also be a relationship between the family liaison strategy and the house-to-house, search and elimination strategies. For example, in a case where it is suspected that someone has been unlawfully killed by a friend of the family during a visit to the victim's residence the following issues may have an impact on the family liaison strategy:

- The overall management of the family liaison is likely to be influenced by the way matters are reported in the media (something that is in part influenced by the media strategy).
- Victimology may be used to identify places where there may have been some contact between the victim and a suspected offender and this may have an impact on the forensic and search strategies.
- Some of the questions asked during the house-to-house enquiries may be influenced by what victimology enquiries establish about the victim's lifestyle and the suspected offender's visiting habits.
- The family liaison strategy may include objectives intended to identify members of the family who might be in a position to provide circumstantial witness evidence to the interview team that either implicates or exonerates a suspected offender.

A family liaison strategy consists of:

- setting and prioritizing a series of objectives for the liaison;
- risk assessment;
- specifying the management structures and systems that are necessary to deliver the objectives.

KEY POINT – ELEMENTS OF A FAMILY LIAISON STRATEGY

A family liaison strategy consists of:

- objectives (standard and case-specific);
- priorities;
- risk assessment;
- management structures and systems.

3.2.1 **Objectives**

Family liaison objectives fall into two categories: standard objectives common to every deployment of a family liaison officer and case-specific objectives peculiar to the circumstances of the investigation.

Standard objectives common to every case include:

- to help the family to understand the criminal justice and coronial processes;
- to communicate information concerning the investigation to the family, as directed by the SIO or SIM, in an accurate and timely manner;
- to explain the media strategy for the investigation to the family.

Case-specific objectives should focus on the demands of the investigation while being sensitive to the needs of the family. These objectives may include:

- to ascertain information from the family as tasked by the SIO or SIM and to record it in an appropriate format (*this information should then be listed*);
- to ascertain background information and antecedents from the family with a view to developing a victimology for the deceased (see chapter 5);
- to compile a family tree to help the investigation understand the family structure;
- to obtain a detailed description of all those within the family and anybody else who visits the family home at the same time as the family liaison officer;
- to secure material such as personal records (diaries, bank statements, personal computers, mobile telephones etc.);
- to secure material needed to confirm the identification of the deceased (forensic, photographic etc.).

In each case, family liaison objectives should be clear, precise and achievable. Poorly-framed objectives are likely to lead to the family liaison officer having a lack of clarity about their purpose, the consequences of which may be a lack of understanding on the part of the family and the investigative team about what family liaison is actually trying to achieve. In addition to this, it is difficult to be certain when poorly-framed vague objectives have been achieved. Given that the achievement of case-specific objectives mark when the task is complete, such a lack of clarity is likely to give rise to some uncertainty about the most appropriate time for the family liaison officer to exit from their role with the family.

Having specified the objectives for family liaison, the SIO or SIM should prioritize them. This is essential because prioritization provides the basis for directing the order in which a family liaison officer should perform the tasks derived from the objectives. For example, in homicide cases in which it is suspected that the deceased's financial affairs may have been a motivating factor it would obviously make sense for an objective relating to their income, outgoings, monetary transactions, purchases, loans and other debts, credit cards and gambling habits (if any) to be a priority for the family liaison officer. Alternatively, victimology may be less of a priority where there are serious concerns about the potential impact of the family speaking to the press outside the scope of the media strategy for the investigation; in these circumstances an explanation to the family of the rationale for the media strategy and the potential consequences on any subsequent legal proceedings of going beyond it will obviously be more of a priority.

A failure on the part of the SIO or SIM to direct the family liaison officer as to the priorities for the investigation is likely to lead to family liaison officers having to make their own assumptions about those priorities. Given that the family liaison officer will not necessarily have the same broad knowledge of the investigation as the SIO or SIM, it is unrealistic to assume that their priorities will necessarily be the same as those of the investigation.

3.2.2 **Risk assessment**

After prioritizing the objectives, the SIO or SIM should conduct a risk assessment before selecting a family liaison officer.

While all family liaison officers should be properly selected, trained and competent, the objectives and the risk assessment should be used in conjunction with the circumstances of the family concerned to inform the most appropriate choice of officer for the particular case under investigation.

SIOs and SIMs have a duty of care to family liaison officers; such a duty of care is partially discharged by developing a risk assessment. It should be borne in mind that risk assessment is a dynamic process that is subject to change as the circumstances of the investigation change and as family liaison develops. It is, therefore, very important not to see risk assessment as a one-off procedure to be completed at the start of the investigation; it is very much an ongoing process that needs to be managed throughout the period during which family liaison is in place.

In essence, a risk assessment for family liaison purposes amounts to considering:

- the people with whom liaison is to take place;
- the place in which liaison is to be conducted;
- the nature of the task demanded of the family liaison officer.

The people with whom the liaison is to take place are obviously the family. It must, however, be established which people constitute the family and the nature of the relationships between them. For example, it may be that the 'family' unit is confined to one or two parents and a few children; alternatively the 'family' may include members of the extended family or friends of the family either living at the same address or frequently visiting it. Similarly, relationships within the family may have a rigid hierarchical structure or they may be flexible in their nature. As much of this information should, ideally, be established before family liaison commences, although in practice it is likely that some of it can only be developed by the family liaison officer following initial contact.

The place at which liaison is to take place will usually be the family address. The general environment in which the address is located should be considered as part of the risk assessment. For example, the manner in which the family liaison officer travels to and from the address may be affected if the locality in which it is situated is a high-crime area where the police are seldom welcome and intimidation is rife. The address itself should also be considered given that the family liaison officer is likely to need to spend a great deal of time there. For example, if the address is particularly overcrowded and the occupants have nowhere else to go, it may be necessary to find an alternative venue when the family liaison officer needs to perform some of the sensitive tasks, such as those associated with establishing aspects of the lifestyle of the deceased that the family may not be cognisant of or comfortable about.

The objectives determine the nature of the family liaison officer's task in the family. In most instances this is unlikely to be the source of any friction between them but in some cases it will. Such a source of friction may arise relatively early in the investigation where the family liaison officer is, for example, tasked to elicit information from the family in respect of an aspect of the deceased's life that they are likely to consider will bring shame on the family. Alternatively, it may be that the need to tackle sensitive issues emerges later on in the enquiry, for example where it is subsequently believed that a member of the family might be involved in the death in some way.

Having obtained as much information as possible about the people and the place where the liaison will be conducted and having thought about the tasks set for the family liaison officer, the SIO or SIM will need to consider the nature of any potential risk and the chances of harm actually occurring. Having thought about these issues the SIO or SIM should then consider what, if anything, could reduce the risk occurring or the severity of its impact if it does.

3.2.3 **Management structures and systems**

At the same time as selecting the most appropriate officer, the SIO or the SIM should establish the reporting structure for family liaison. In many instances, this might be to report to and be tasked by the SIO or SIM, or their deputy, personally. In cases such as mass disaster that merit the deployment of a large number of family liaison officers, however, the SIM might ask individual officers to report to a nominated coordinator. Whatever the decision of the SIO or the SIM, a clear reporting structure is essential to ensure that family liaison progresses as smoothly as possible in the context of an investigation.

3.2.4 **Briefing the Family liaison officer**

The final component of this initial stage of the family liaison strategy is to brief the family liaison officer. Such a briefing should consist of the following:

- the circumstances of the case under investigation as they are known at the time of the briefing;
- the circumstances of the family as known at the time of the briefing;
- the reporting structure for family liaison in the investigation;
- the objectives and the SIO or SIM's prioritization of those objectives.

The briefing should also cover the SIO or SIM's expectations of the family liaison officer. Such expectations include:

- to communicate any information from the family to the investigation team in an accurate and timely manner;

- to identify any significant witnesses within the family to the investigation team as soon as possible (see chapter 6);
- to report any concerns that the family have about the investigation to the SIO or SIM, in an accurate and timely manner;
- to report any deterioration in the quality of their relationship with the family to the SIO or SIM as soon as possible.

KEY POINT – BRIEFING FOR FAMILY LIAISON OFFICERS

A briefing for family liaison officers by the SIO or SIM should include the following:

- the circumstances of the case under investigation;
- anything that is already known about the family of the deceased;
- the objectives of the deployment;
- the priorities for the investigation;
- the name of the supervisor to whom the family liaison officer should report;
- the need to notify the investigation of any significant witnesses in the family as soon as possible;
- the need to report in a timely manner any:
  - information that the family has for the investigation team;
  - concerns that the family has about the investigation;
  - deterioration in the family liaison officer's relationship with the family.

Following the briefing, responsibility falls to the family liaison officer to develop a plan for initial contact with the family.

3.2.5 Records

A written record of the family liaison strategy should be maintained by the SIO or the SIM, or by a family liaison coordinator or a family liaison adviser appointed to act on their behalf. It is difficult to provide an example of a family liaison strategy because the circumstances in which family liaison takes place differ so widely. The following example might, however, be useful provided that it is viewed as a highly context-specific illustration rather than as a template.

Example — family liaison strategy

The objectives for family liaison for this investigation are as follows:

- to help the family to understand the criminal justice and coronial processes;
- to communicate information concerning the investigation to the family, as directed by the SIO or SIM, in an accurate and timely manner;

- to explain the media strategy for the investigation to the family;
- to construct a family tree;
- to obtain a detailed description of all those within the family and anybody else who visits the family home at the same time as the family liaison officer;
- to obtain details of the victim's usual routines, including any routes normally taken to work or for leisure activities;
- to obtain details of all the victim's friends and acquaintances (current and over the last five years);
- to obtain details of the victim's finances including:
  - income (taxed or otherwise);
  - outgoings (food, rent, utilities);
  - savings;
  - loans and other debts;
  - spending habits (leisure, entertainment, holidays, gambling);
- secure diaries, address books, bank statements, personal computers and mobile telephones.

The immediate priorities in respect of victimology for this investigation are:

- to obtain details of all the victim's current friends and acquaintances;
- to obtain details of the victim's finances with particular emphasis on their spending and gambling habits;
- to secure diaries, address books, bank statements, personal computers and mobile telephones.

Additional priorities will be set when the tasks in respect of the immediate priorities have been completed.

Initial enquiries suggest that the 'family' in this case only consists of the wife of the deceased and their two children. In addition to this, the deceased's only surviving parent is his mother, whom he regularly visited. It is not known if he had any siblings.

See the risk assessment forms.

Preliminary information about the family and its composition and the nature of the tasks to be completed suggest that the most appropriate family liaison officers for this dual deployment are [*name*] and [*name*]; they have now been briefed and deployed in this role.

3.3 **Family Liaison Plans**

Family liaison officers are responsible for day-to-day contact with the family. Such contact invariably requires a degree of planning. Planning must take account of the SIO or SIM's family liaison strategy.

A plan for initial contact focuses on the tactical issues involved in communicating with the family during the first visit to their home. Some research on the part of the family liaison officer is essential before developing such a plan. This research should include:

- clarifying any gaps in their understanding of what is known about the circumstances of the incident (including how the incident became known to the police). This kind of information is likely to be available within the investigation team;
- the current situation in respect of the investigation;
- finding out as much as possible about the family, including friends, associates and anybody else known to regularly frequent the family's address. This kind of information is likely to be available from local and national police records, local police sources and, if applicable, social services departments;
- finding out as much as possible about the community within which the family live. This kind of information is likely to be available from local police sources;
- establishing the extent and nature of contact between the family and the police since the incident, including what information has been passed to them. This kind of information is likely to be available from officers who first attended the incident and the investigative team;
- finding out how the family and the community in which they live have reacted or are likely to react to the incident. This kind of information is likely to be available from officers who first attended the incident and the investigative team;
- establishing what information concerning the incident is already in the public domain, including the media. This kind of information is likely to be available from local police sources and police media specialists.

If any of this information has an impact on the risk assessment it should be brought to the attention of the SIO or SIM.

Such information should then be used to plan the initial contact with the family. Initial contact with the family should consist of:

- explaining the roles of the family liaison officer and the SIO or SIM and letting the family know how they can be contacted;
- providing appropriate information to the family in respect of what is known about the circumstances of the death;
- explaining the coroner's processes, including the post-mortem;
- listening to the family's views about what has happened and any opinions that they have about the investigation;
- obtaining an overview of the composition of the family and anybody else living at the address or frequenting it;
- identifying the main point of contact within the family;
- encouraging the family to seek medical advice, if appropriate (eg as a result of the impact of trauma);
- encouraging the family to seek support from local support groups, if appropriate;

- explaining the media strategy for the investigation;
- obtaining any initial material from the family as directed by the SIO or SIM (in accordance with the tasks arising from the prioritized objectives);
- starting to develop a victimology, as directed by the SIO or SIM.

The development of a plan for initial contact with the family is summarized below.

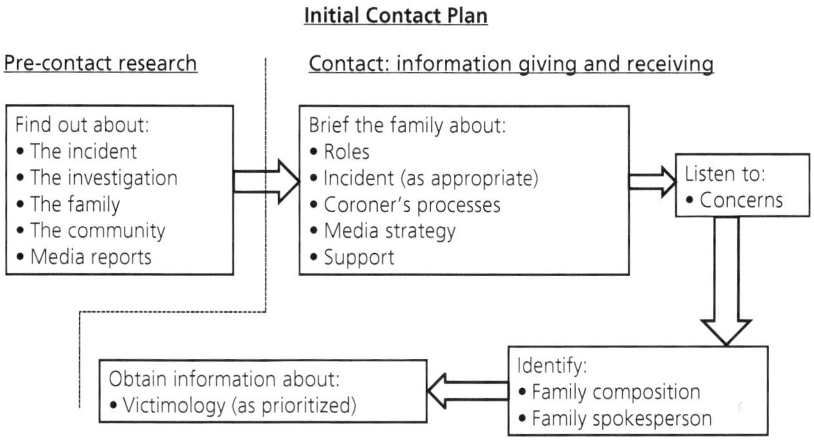

Figure 3.1 Initial contact plan

In essence, a plan for initial contact with the family should determine the most appropriate method for approaching them and managing their expectations, while taking account of the risk assessment and allowing for the necessary flexibility.

3.4 Chapter Summary

This chapter has identified the various components of a family liaison strategy and a family liaison plan in the context of initial contact with the family. Strategies are high level overviews that govern the direction of family liaison in the context of the wider investigation, whereas plans focus on the tactical considerations involved in communicating with the family on a day-to-day basis. The SIO or SIM is responsible for the strategy and the family liaison officer is responsible for the plan.

Family liaison strategies consist of developing and prioritizing a series of objectives, then establishing the management structures and systems that are necessary for their delivery.

Strategies should influence the selection of the most appropriate family liaison officer.

Family liaison strategies should be included in the briefing given to the family liaison officer. The first step in developing a plan involves obtaining the necessary information about the circumstances of the investigation and trying to find out as much as possible about the family. The second step in developing the plan involves bringing such information to bear on determining the structure and the content of the initial contact with the family.

NOTES

NOTES

NOTES

4

The Management and Coordination of Family Liaison

4.1 Introduction

Given that communication is the essence of family liaison, the management and coordination of family liaison is very much an exercise in the management and coordination of communication. The relationship between the police and the family is a direct one in most investigations. In some investigations the relationship is less straightforward in that communication takes place via a third party representing the family. In either event, communication in the context of family liaison is a two-way process in which the family and the investigation team want information from each other.

This chapter discusses the issues involved in communicating with the family. It looks at direct and indirect communication between the family and the police and considers how their differing information requirements may be managed.

4.2 Communicating with the Family

Families usually want to know about a number of things including the circumstances in which the death took place, the progress of the investigation, when they can make arrangements for the funeral and when they can expect to receive a death certificate.

KEY POINT – WHAT FAMILIES USUALLY WANT TO KNOW

Families usually want to know:

- circumstances of the death;
- progress of the investigation;
- when they can arrange the funeral.

Details of the circumstances of the death and the progress of the investigation should only be provided as directed by the SIO or the SIM. The timing of the release of the body should be discussed with the coroner's officer.

Information concerning what is known about the circumstances of the death and the progress of the investigation should only be passed to the family under the specific directions of the senior investigating officer (SIO) of the investigation or, in the case of a mass disaster, the senior identification manager (SIM). The SIO or the SIM should ensure that as much information as possible is passed to the family, only withholding details that could compromise the investigation in the event of them becoming more widely known. Information concerning the coronial process may be obtained from the coroner's officer. Any information given by the family liaison officer to the family should be as accurate and up-to-date as possible.

Scheduled contact between the family liaison officer and the family should be planned. This includes visits to the family home and anticipated telephone contact. Such planning should begin by establishing developments since the last contact. It should focus on developments in the:

- investigation;
- family circumstances;
- media coverage;
- community tension.

4.3 Family Liaison Interviews

Most scheduled contact between the family liaison officer and the family should involve pursuing the objectives set by the SIO or the SIM. As noted in chapter 3, Initial Contact with the Family, some of these objectives will be standard in the sense of being common to every case in which family liaison takes place and others will be case-specific. Scheduled contact between the family liaison officer and the family may focus on either standard or case-specific objectives, or a combination of the two. All scheduled contact with the family should be planned, regardless of which objectives are pursued.

The nature of standard objectives is such that they tend to involve the family liaison officer providing information to the family. In these circumstances, it is important for the family liaison officer to identify the most appropriate person to receive that information on behalf of the family, particularly when liaising with a large family.

On the other hand, the nature of case-specific objectives is such that they tend to involve the family providing information and other material to the investigation team via the family liaison officer. In these circumstances, the contact can be said to amount to an interview.

4.4 Family Liaison Interview Strategies

In complex cases where a need has been identified by the SIO or the SIM for some information from the family that might be of central importance to the investigation, some thought could be given to developing a family liaison interview strategy.

There is potential for some confusion about the difference between a family liaison interview strategy and a family liaison interview plan, to the extent that the terms might end up being used interchangeably. For the sake of clarity, this chapter considers a strategy to be a high level overview of the family liaison interviews in the wider context of the overall family liaison strategy and the investigation, whereas a plan focuses on the tactical considerations applicable to individual family liaison interviews. While family liaison interview strategies and plans are mutually dependent on each other, they are separate entities in their own right. Responsibility for a family liaison interview strategy usually falls to the family liaison coordinator, family liaison adviser or an interview adviser appointed by the SIO or the SIM (see *National Investigative Interviewing Strategy* (Association of Chief Police Officers, 2009) for more on the role of an interview adviser). Responsibility for family liaison interview plans falls to the family liaison officer.

4.4.1 **Components of a family liaison interview strategy**

The processes and contents of a family liaison interview strategy may be represented by the following diagram:

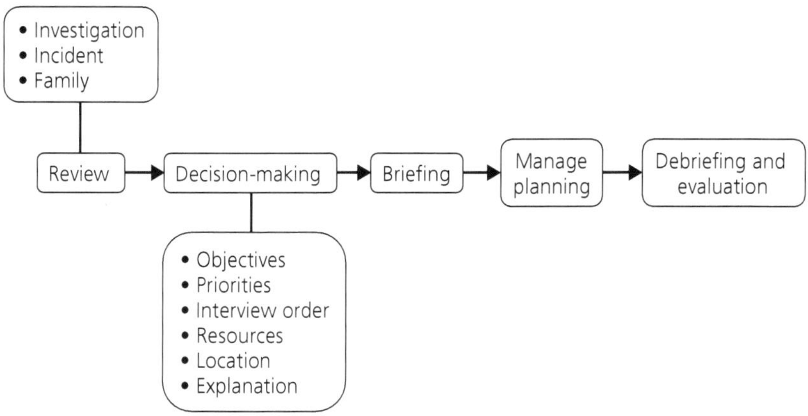

Figure 4.1 The processes and components of a family liaison interview strategy

As suggested in this diagram, a family liaison interview strategy may be broken down into a number of phases. While these phases are in principle sequential, in practice some of them can overlap.

4.4.1.1 **Phase 1: review**

Prior to making decisions about a family liaison interview strategy, as much as possible of the material already gathered by the investigation and anything that is being said about it in the public domain should be reviewed. The review should include the material referred to in the previous chapter (chapter 3, Initial Contact with the Family), particularly:

- what is known about the family;
- what is known about the circumstances of the death that is being investigated;
- how the death that is being investigated came to the attention of the police;
- the general progress of the investigation to date, including current and proposed future lines of enquiry;

- the background material considered to be important to the investigation and the priorities for obtaining it.

Consideration should also be given to the potential impact of the other aspects of the investigation on the family liaison interview process. These other aspects of the investigation could include the:

- forensic strategy;
- identification strategy;
- media strategy;
- arrest strategy.

4.4.1.2 **Phase 2: decisions**

A number of decisions then need to be made on the basis of the review, including:

- the objectives of the interviews;
- the order in which people within the family are to be interviewed;
- the resources required to conduct the interviews;
- the location for the interviews;
- how the reason for the interview is to be explained to the family.

4.4.2 **The objectives of the family liaison interviews**

The objectives of a family liaison interview are likely to be concentrated into two areas:

- circumstantial material surrounding the death (eg an account of the last time that the deceased was seen alive by the family);
- victimology relating to various aspects of the deceased's life style (eg relationships, spending habits).

Objectives for the interview that focus on these two areas should be developed. Such objectives should be framed as clearly and precisely as possible so that family liaison officers can understand what is required by the investigation.

4.4.2.1 **Prioritize the objectives**

Having set the objectives, it is necessary to list them in order of priority. Unless this is done the investigation team will not necessarily get the information that they require as quickly as they need it and this may lead to other potentially less fruitful lines of enquiry being pursued, needlessly delaying the successful resolution of the enquiry.

4.4.2.2 **The order of the interviews**

A family liaison interview strategy usually needs to consider the order in which the interviews are to take place. For example, it may be that in some cases the first interviewee is the person likely to provide the most relevant information while in other cases the availability of individual family members or cultural rules governing precedence may influence the decision regardless of who is likely to provide the most relevant information.

4.4.2.3 **The resources required to conduct the interviews**

Consideration should be given to the resources required to conduct the interviews in terms of the number of family liaison officers. The number of family liaison officers needed depends on:

- the priority for and urgency of the information required; and
- the size of the family.

In taking account of the priority for and urgency of the information required, the resources needed may vary from objective to objective. For example, it may be that several family liaison officers could be deployed if information about the deceased's relationships within a big family are required as a matter of urgency, but that the number of family liaison officers required decreases when low-priority broader information about the deceased's spending habits is to be obtained.

In addition to consideration of the number of family liaison officers required to interview the family, some thought will also need to be given to interpreters and intermediaries where necessary (see chapter 6 for more about intermediaries).

4.4.2.4 **The location for the interviews**

Though most family liaison interviews take place in the family home, it should not be assumed that it is appropriate to conduct every interview in this way. There may be occasions when the nature of the topic that is the focus of the interview, or distractions such as noise and activity within the family home, are such as to make the home an entirely inappropriate location for the interview. In these circumstances it will be necessary to identify another quieter, more private, location such as a police interview suite.

4.4.2.5 **Consider how the reason for the interview is to be explained to the family**

In most instances an explanation to the family for needing to interview them about a particular topic will present little problem. The fact that this is not always the case, however, means that it is important to consider how the interview is to be explained to the family within the family liaison interview strategy. Instances where an explanation to the family might not be straightforward include:

- situations in which sensitive issues, such as the sexual habits of the deceased or behaviour that might be regarded as socially unacceptable on the part of the deceased (eg drug taking, gambling), are to be the focus of the interview;

- situations in which family suspicions as to the identity of the suspected offender or the circumstances of the death might be encouraged by the focus of the interview (eg unless it is explained properly and done sensitively, asking the family about the quality of the deceased's relationship with their spouse might give rise to a suspicion on the part of the family that the investigation team think the spouse is responsible for the death).

4.4.2.6 **Brief the family liaison officers**

The family liaison coordinator, family liaison adviser or the interview adviser responsible for the family liaison interview strategy should brief the family liaison officers as soon as possible. This briefing should include:

- the objectives for the family liaison interviews;
- the priority for each objective;
- the order in which members of the family should be approached in respect of the interviews;
- the resources allocated to achieve the objectives;
- any decisions as to the location of the family liaison interviews;
- how the reason for the interviews is to be explained to the family.

4.4.2.7 **Manage the planning process**

The family liaison coordinator, family liaison adviser or the interview adviser responsible for the family liaison interview strategy should manage the family liaison officers' preparation of the interview plan. This involves:

- ensuring that the topics to be covered are detailed, meaningful and consistent with the objectives;
- assisting with the structure of the interviews, including the sequencing of the topics;
- agreeing how the topics are to be introduced if they relate to issues that the family might regard as sensitive;
- agreeing appropriate tactics for dealing with any potential barriers to communication.

4.4.2.8 **Debrief the family liaison officers and evaluate their interviews**

The family liaison coordinator, family liaison adviser or the interview adviser responsible for the family liaison interview strategy should debrief the family liaison officers and review their records of the interviews to assess the information from the family in the context of the broader investigation, particularly in terms of:

- what it tells the investigative team about the alleged event;
- what fresh lines of enquiry arise from it;
- whether there are any gaps in the family's information; and

- whether there are any inconsistencies in the family's information and other material obtained during the course of the investigation.

This information should then be passed to and if necessary discussed with the SIO, SIM or nominated member of the investigative team.

If the family liaison interviews have proved challenging the family liaison coordinator, family liaison adviser or the interview adviser should bring it to the attention of the SIO or the SIM with a view to considering its implications for the deployment (ie whether the deployment should continue or whether it might be appropriate to deploy another family liaison officer).

4.5 Family Liaison Interview Plans

The planning for a family liaison interview should take account of:

- the tasks derived from the prioritized standard and case-specific objectives set by the SIO or the SIM (see chapter 3, Initial Contact with the Family);
- which particular members of the family are most likely to be able to provide the material necessary to complete the task at hand;
- the structure and content of the communication;
- record keeping.

4.5.1 Tasks

A number of tasks are likely to fall out of the prioritized standard and case-specific objectives set by the SIO or the SIM. For example, the overall aim of developing a victimology is too general to be of much use unless it is divided into a series of precise objectives: even precise objectives can be broken down into a number of topics that form a series of tasks. For example, victimology might include the deceased's finances; the deceased's finances might include a number of topics such as income, outgoings, bank accounts, savings and debt.

4.5.2 Members of the family

Where more than one member of the family is likely to be able to provide the material necessary to complete a task it will not usually be appropriate to interview them together since the process of doing so could inhibit and contaminate memory recall. Given these circumstances, the family liaison officer will need to determine the most appropriate order to interview different members of the family. This is likely to be influenced by a number of factors including:

- cultural considerations;
- the urgency of the task;
- the member of the family likely to be in a position to provide the most useful material;

- the availability of each member of the family likely to be able to provide the material.

4.5.3 **Structure and content**

The structure and content of the interview is likely to be similar to other models of police interviewing. Such models usually begin with establishing a rapport before moving on to eliciting and clarifying an account, and then end with some kind of closure followed by an evaluation of the content and quality of the interaction. In the UK these models are characterized by the mnemonics PEACE (**P**lanning and preparation, **E**ngage and explain, **A**ccount, **C**losure and **E**valuation) and PRICE (**P**reparation, **R**apport, **I**nformation, **C**onfirmation and **E**valuation), or the structure set out for witness interviewing in *Achieving Best Evidence in Criminal Proceedings: Guidance for Interviewing Victims and Witnesses, and Using Special Measures* (Office for Criminal Justice Reform, 2007). Outside the UK these models may use different terms for each phase but the framework in which they are set amounts to the same or a similar thing.

KEY POINT – PEACE AND PRICE INTERVIEW FRAMEWORKS	
Preparation and planning	**P**reparation
Engage and explain	**R**apport
Account	**I**nformation
Closure	**C**onfirmation
Evaluation	**E**valuation

The structure of a family liaison interview can be characterized as:

- Rapport (or engage and explain);
- Account;
- Clarification;
- Information important to the investigation;
- Closure;
- Evaluation.

This framework is illustrated in Figure 4.2

4.5.3.1 **Rapport**

The rapport phase of a family liaison interview may be further divided into:

- soliciting information; and
- imparting information.

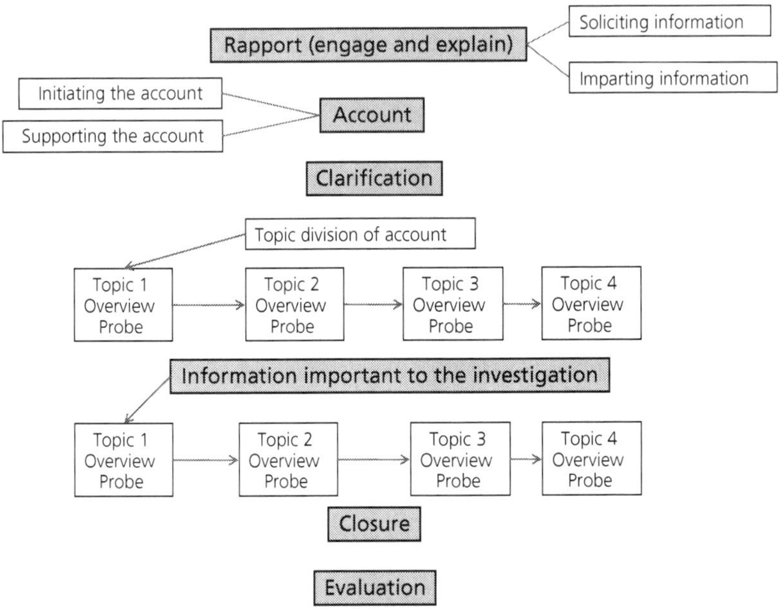

Figure 4.2 The structure of a family liaison interview

Soliciting information from a member of the family during the rapport phase usually consists of asking them what developments there have been since they last spoke to the family liaison officer. Some such developments might warrant further action such as encouraging the family to seek medical assistance, explaining the investigative or coronial processes, or referring them to the coroner's officer or seeking guidance from the SIO or the SIM.

Imparting information to the family refers to updating them on the progress of the investigation (as directed by the SIO or the SIM) and any issues arising in the media or wider community.

4.5.3.2 **Account**

Accounts may be either incident-based as in, for example, a family liaison officer's role in trying to establish the circumstances surrounding a sudden infant death, or they may have a lifestyle focus as in, for example, trying to find out which places the deceased regularly frequented. The account phase of a family liaison interview consists of the following elements:

- initiating the account (eg 'tell me about [the deceased's] financial situation'); and
- supporting the account (eg questions that echo the words used by the interviewee such as 'he had a current account in Barclays?' and follow-up questions intended to keep the account going like 'what did [the deceased] do about that?').

4.5.3.3 **Clarification of the account**

This part of the interview includes:

- division of the interviewee's account into manageable topics;
- systematic development and clarification of the topics that make up the account by:
  - eliciting an overview or mini-account that covers the topic area by means of an open-ended invitation (eg questions beginning with 'tell me', 'explain to me' or 'describe to me'); and then
  - probing the topic area by means of a combination of open-ended and specific-closed questions (eg questions beginning with 'what', 'where', when', 'who', 'why', and 'how').

4.5.3.4 **Information important to the investigation**

Having developed the interviewee's account it may then be necessary to consider any other information important to the investigation that has not already been covered in the interview. For example, if intelligence obtained during the general course of the investigation suggests that the victim of a homicide might have been involved in a great deal of gambling, and this cannot be ruled out as a motive for murder, it may be appropriate sensitively to probe this aspect of the victim's lifestyle even though it has not already been remarked upon in the interviewee's account.

4.5.3.5 **Closure**

Closure consists of summarizing the interviewee's account, unless it is inappropriate to do so, thanking the interviewee and giving them some indication about what is likely to happen next (eg 'I'm going to let the investigation team know about this and they'll follow it up if need be').

4.5.3.6 **Evaluation**

As with any other police interview, family liaison interviews should be followed by a period of reflection in which the interviewer considers the material provided during the interview in terms of:

- any immediate follow-up activity required; and
- how the account fits in with any other material known to the family liaison officer.

The family liaison officer should then brief the SIO, the SIM or their nominee about the material they have obtained.

Finally, the family liaison officer should reflect on their performance during the interview with a view to making any improvements necessary in the future.

4.5.4. **Record keeping**

It is essential that family liaison officers, at the earliest opportunity, make a full record of any contact or attempted contact with the family, including any interview. Failure to make and retain such records could leave the reliability of the family liaison officer's testimony open to challenge at a later stage in the investigative or judicial process.

4.6 Indirect Communication with the Family

While direct communication between the family liaison officer and the family is the usual and certainly the most desirable state of affairs, because it is likely to maximize investigative opportunities by optimizing the flow of information from the family and enhancing confidence in the investigation, it should be acknowledged that this is not always going to be the case. Some families may find it hard to communicate with the police for a variety of reasons, including adverse perceptions of the police based on experience or popular perception within their community.

In these circumstances where it is difficult to establish or maintain direct communication with the family, advice from those who understand the community, within the police service and the community at large, may prove crucial. In some instances this might include encouraging members of the community to form an independent advisory group to provide guidance for the SIO or the SIM as they develop their family liaison strategy and the family liaison officer as they plan their communication with the family. See *Family Liaison Officers Manual* (ACPO, 2008) for further information about independent advisory groups.

In some cases, the family might find it easier to communicate with the investigation team through a representative (often though not always a legal adviser, eg a solicitor) and they should not be discouraged from doing so.

The involvement of a representative should not be seen as an impervious barrier to communicating with the family. The SIO or the SIM and the family liaison officer should do their utmost to work with the representative to ensure that the flow of information between the investigation team and the family is as effective as possible.

4.7 Exit Strategies

As an investigation progresses there is danger that the family will become too dependent on the family liaison officer and the family liaison officer too dependent on the family. Such dependence can have an adverse effect on the family, the family liaison officer and the investigation. For this reason, the SIO or the

SIM should consider implementing an exit strategy for the family liaison officer as soon as the family liaison objectives have been achieved. Such a strategy should include the nomination of a contact officer for the family who is responsible for bringing any concerns they might have to the attention of the SIO or the SIM and for relaying any information about developments in the case to the family as directed by the SIO or the SIM. An exit strategy should also make provision for the family to familiarize themselves with the court before any trial that might take place in connection with the death.

KEY POINT - EXIT STRATEGIES

An exit strategy should:

- be implemented when the objectives set out in the family liaison strategy have been achieved;
- include the nomination of a contact officer to provide an ongoing link between the family and the investigation;
- provide the family with an opportunity to familiarize themselves with the court before any trial takes place in respect of the death.

The successful implementation of an exit strategy is likely to be facilitated by:

- a well-timed personal visit to the family from the SIO or the SIM and the family liaison officer during which the information about the exit strategy is sensitively delivered;
- the final debriefing of the family liaison officer by the SIO or the SIM;
- the briefing of the contact officer by the SIO or the SIM.

4.8 Chapter Summary

This chapter has set out to describe the processes involved in the ongoing management and coordination of family liaison. In considering these issues the chapter has focused on the importance of planned communication with the family and introduced the concept of a family liaison interview. While most of the chapter is dedicated to direct communication between the family liaison officer and the family, because this is the mode of contact between the family and the investigation in the vast majority of investigations, it has also acknowledged that challenges sometimes arise that lead to indirect communication via a representative of the family. Finally, the chapter has considered the importance of implementing an exit strategy as soon as the objectives set for family liaison have been met.

NOTES

5

Victimology

5.1 Introduction

It is important at the start of this chapter to state clearly the context within which the word 'victimology' is used in police family liaison, because there are a number of interpretations of it in current use.

Only a small percentage of people who are killed by an illegal act have had no previous contact with their killer. The very nature of homicide is that it is normally an act of violence, an act premeditated by some form of aggression that causes one person to kill another. At the outset of an investigation much can be gained from the scene itself. It bears testimony to what took place there. Crime scene investigation (CSI) has always been of enormous value, and as science and technology make advances CSI becomes more and more sophisticated at establishing forensic links between killer, scene and victim. It is, however, the case that while CSI can often tell investigators *what* took place it can never tell them *why*.

The nature of the crime itself will often tell investigators something about the person who committed it and generate many lines of enquiry. Local enquiries around the scene may identify potential witnesses or sightings of people acting suspiciously. If investigators are lucky, there may even be an eyewitness.

Extensive 'house-to-house' enquiries are standard practice in these situations, and parameters are set in the hope of obtaining information that can assist the investigation. Leaflet drops and poster campaigns are used to increase public awareness of the crime, to help jog people's memory and to encourage people with any possible information to come forward. Police will often set up cordons to appeal to any members of the public who may have been in the area at the time of the crime or who may have passed through the area at a similar hour or day on a previous occasion.

Databases are searched for crimes and injuries that are of a similar nature to the murder, and at some stage hopefully a suspect or suspects may begin to emerge, which will generate further lines of enquiry relating to their movements and behaviour at the time of the crime. Ultimately if the right suspects emerge from these enquiries and they are interviewed and forensically examined then the combination of CSI, local enquiries, specialist advice, high quality witness interviews and committed, smart detective work will be enough to deliver a case file that can be successfully prosecuted.

There is, however, one essential element that has not been mentioned above, and that is the influence that the victim(s) themselves may have on the successful investigation of the crime committed against them. Of all the witnesses that could be considered 'significant' to an investigation, in types of crime other than homicide the victim scores highest. If an assault, a serious sexual offence, a burglary or even a fraud is being investigated the victim is an absolutely central witness and has to be interviewed as soon as possible and often at great length.

In a homicide it is obviously not possible to interview the victim. A 'reconstruction' of the victim's life or lifestyle, therefore, has to take place. The best way to do that is to identify and interview those who know most about the victim. The purpose of this chapter is not to describe every avenue of investigation in depth, but to show where 'victimology' sits and why it should be central to a major crime enquiry. The effective family liaison officer will be able to work with a family even when they are experiencing the most unbearable emotional pain and conduct high quality interviews with them to set the foundations of what should become a wider 'victimology' strategy.

KEY POINT – VICTIMOLOGY

In the context of police family liaison, 'victimology' refers to a number of factors that make up the deceased's life or lifestyle. These factors include their routines, finances, behaviour, relationships, geographical movements and the precursor events that led up to their death. The development of a victimology amounts to a reconstruction of the deceased's life.

5.2 Three Variables

Every time someone is killed by a criminal act, several dynamic variables need to come together. They are:

- the suspect(s);
- the scene of the crime;
- the victim of the crime.

As a general rule, when someone is killed both the suspect and the victim are usually near or next to each other at the scene of the crime. As with any general rule, there are of course a few exceptions to this, for example an assassination by means of a sniper shot. But the general principle that the suspect is usually next to their victim at the scene of crime remains intact because the exceptions to it are relatively rare. Whenever a killing takes place a scene or several scenes of crime are created. Left at these scenes are potential forensic traces of the suspect and their victim, as well as anybody else's who was present. The links between suspect, scene and victim are illustrated in Figure 5.1.

This chapter will now endeavour to describe these variables in a little more detail, with particular emphasis on the contribution that victimology can make to each of them.

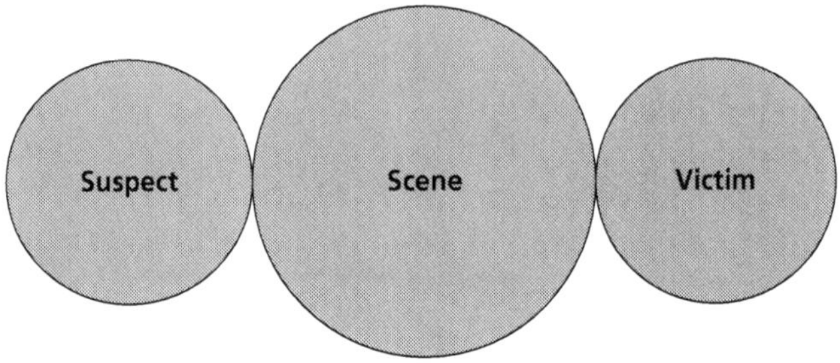

Figure 5.1 Three variables in a homicide

5.3 The Scene

The three main investigative activities that centre on the scene of a crime are:

- crime scene investigation;
- house-to-house enquiries;
- passive data collection, notably CCTV recordings.

Each of these activities contributes toward the development of as comprehensive a picture as possible of what was going on at the scene at the time the killing took place.

5.3.1 Crime scene investigation

The scene of crime takes on substantial significance to investigators, and the initial attending officers at the scene make great efforts to prevent anything being taken away from or added to the scene to avoid the 'contamination' of any evidence collected. The goal of CSI is to establish what the conditions were like at the scene at the time crime occurred. Crime scene investigators seek to answer the question that is at the heart of any investigation: 'what happened here?' At least two other potential investigative processes also come into play when trying to find out what the scene was like at the time the killing took place: house-to-house enquiries and the collection of material from passive data generators.

5.3.2 House-to-house enquiries

The purpose of house-to-house enquiries is to search for possible witnesses as well as to get a snapshot of who lives or works in the area where the crime may have been committed. It is important to remember that someone could have witnessed something that seemed irrelevant at the time that may carry significance when it is considered with other material established during the investigation. This is also a time used to reassure the community and to raise awareness of the incident. The importance of house-to-house enquiries cannot be overstated as many vital clues are often gleaned from this process—eg information about vehicles parked in the area, any recent events that are worthy of further investigation, overheard altercations, door-to-door callers etc.

It is unfortunate that many police media appeals only ask for people who may have witnessed something suspicious to come forward. This amounts to asking people to make a subjective assessment of the relevance of what they have seen before making contact and may result in vital material being lost. An assessment of relevance is something that should be undertaken by investigators. The emphasis in media appeals should, therefore, be on asking people who were in the area on the night to come forward to be interviewed.

This type of work will be backed up by leaflets and posters, to capture any potential witness who is not aware of the investigation. The use of local and sometimes national media can assist in getting appeals for witnesses out.

On certain 'anniversaries' the police may decide to make a larger appeal. One week after the incident is often considered to be a crucial time. Sometimes the police will set up a large-scale enquiry in the area of the scene of crime at around the same time of day as the incident, but a week after the event. This is to find witnesses who are in that area at that time every week. Some of these potential witnesses may only pass that way on that particular day and it is important that the one-week 'anniversary' is dealt with appropriately. If the incident occurred in the early hours of the morning it is possible that by setting up this enquiry at exactly the same time as the crime, witnesses who work late hours—taxi drivers, restaurant workers etc.—may be found.

All this activity is going on in the days and weeks that follow a serious incident and hopefully valuable information is going to be obtained from it.

5.3.3 **Passive data generators**

Passive data generators are defined as 'automated systems that gather and collate information for various purposes' (*Practice Advice on Core Investigative Doctrine* (ACPO, 2005)). There are many kinds of passive data generator and a good investigation will seek to identify all those relevant to the scene of a crime. Of all passive generators, closed-circuit television (CCTV) is usually the most immediate concern to investigators because the recordings may be lost unless they are secured within a relatively short space of time.

Investigators usually try to locate any CCTV images that may be available in the area. These images are important because they can contribute toward an understanding of what was going on at the scene when the killing took place. Figures moving around may be witnesses who need to be traced and their descriptions could be included in media appeals. Images of the location and movement of any vehicles may also generate lines of enquiry by indicating the presence of potential witnesses or, indeed, suspects at or near the scene of the crime.

It is important to remember that CCTV images are not usually kept by the camera owners for ever. The identification of their locations and the early seizure of them by appropriately trained officers is, therefore, as crucial as the recovery of physical evidence from the crime scene. The worst case scenario is that the camera owner is unaware of the importance of that particular day's images and allows them to be recorded over or destroyed.

It is important also that if CCTV is recovered appropriate resources are allocated to their analysis in order that any 'evidence' can be secured and acted upon without delay. The work of Scotland Yard's Counter Terrorism Command stands out in this area when in the aftermath of the 7 July 2005 bombings in London, high priority was placed on the importance of these images in finding out 'what happened here?'

5.4 **The Suspect**

In the early stages of an investigation many crimes do not have an obvious suspect. On these occasions the police will be hoping that witnesses can shed some light on the circumstances surrounding the crime. For example, if a vehicle has been seen in the area by witnesses great efforts will be made to trace vehicles of a similar description and to interview their owners. Without specific vehicle information this can be a laborious task requiring many officers all over the UK tracing and interviewing potential witnesses.

CCTV also has the potential to generate lines of enquiry to trace people or vehicles that may have been at the crime scene when the killing took place. At this stage unless there is strong supporting evidence to the contrary the person leading the investigation will look upon these people as potential witnesses in the investigation who should be interviewed. The content of those interviews should be evaluated and added to everything else that is known. On some occasions while not declaring an individual to be a suspect in the enquiry it may be important to 'eliminate' someone from the investigation and a request will be made to officers to trace, interview and eliminate (TIE) an individual. This can sometimes be done when a simple corroborated check on someone's whereabouts at the time the crime was committed can be established or where a description or DNA sample can easily indicate that the person is not involved in the commission of the crime.

Other avenues will be looked at—the nature of the crime, the circumstances of its commission. Sometimes these areas will highlight individuals who will need to be looked at further. For example, a person who has previous convictions for street robbery cannot be ignored if the nature of the crime indicates that a street robbery was taking place when the crime occurred. Similar considerations apply in respect of people who have previous convictions for burglary, domestic violence, racist offences etc. when the circumstances indicate that these crimes may be a feature of the matter under investigation. If people with convictions for similar offences are locally based it would be negligent of the police service not to give this some priority.

The relationship between the three areas in Figure 5.1 is also an important consideration. For example, suspicions may be heightened if the individual being looked at by the investigation has knowledge of or access to the crime scene or the area surrounding it. In these circumstances, however, it is important to bear in mind that, while having the capability or wherewithal to commit a serious crime is a necessary factor, it is not in itself sufficient: a suspect must have had the opportunity to be in the proximity of the victim at that time.

5.5 The Victim

Statistics are patchy but it seems reasonable to say that in cases of homicide, an attack by a total 'stranger' is very rare. Research tends to suggest that homicides are usually committed by someone who has had some sort of previous interaction with the victim. Most crime statistics do not, however, capture things like, 'were at the same school at the same time, lives in the same neighbourhood and encounters the victim during a shared routine, drinks in the same pub on a regular basis, purchased a used car from them, travels to work on the same train every day etc.'

If we were able to capture and evaluate that kind of vague or indefinable 'relationship' at the end of an investigation it seems likely that the percentage of total stranger homicides would be very low indeed. Recreating the victim's lifestyle and routine can be of enormous value even where the victim was unaware of the presence of the suspect, because the suspect would have been involved in their daily life in some way when the crime occurred. While the question is still 'what happened here', in developing a victimology, we are adding context and circumstance to the other parts of Figure 5.1 (ie the crime scene and the suspect enquiries). Figure 5.2 is a pictorial representation of the various aspects of a person's life that contribute toward a victimology. The victim is always the central point or 'nominal one' around which the victimology is developed.

Figure 5.2 outlines areas of victim information that investigators may want to develop. It should be stressed, however, that the prioritization of these areas needs to be managed by the person who knows most about the investigation—the SIO or the SIM. For example, during the investigation into the murder by Steve Wright of five women who were working as prostitutes in Ipswich in November/December 2006 it was a victimology priority to trace associates of the deceased so that their routines could be established with a view to fully investigating any precursor events. In addition to this, by understanding the victims' routines it could be established that the locations in which their bodies were found were not places that they would have chosen to take clients. It is, therefore, the case that even negative information can tell investigators something; if the deceased did not choose the locations the murderer surely did.

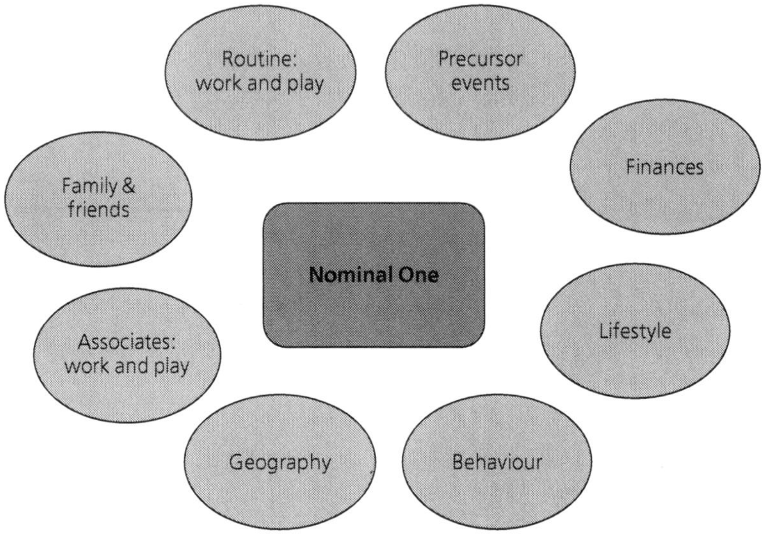

Figure 5.2 Victimology

5.5.1 **Precursor events**

Precursor events can be very important because murders tend to occur between people with 'history'. The murder itself may be the culmination of a dispute that has been going on for some time. This could be a financial arrangement, a business deal, a criminal activity or a personal relationship that has gone wrong.

When family liaison officers are working with families they have to be able to conduct the type of interviews that will allow the family and friends to describe the murdered person's life. Questions like, 'Did they have any enemies?' are far too closed and could yield one-word replies. In addition to this, the family may not be aware of a concealed animosity between the deceased and some of the people with whom they associated because they may have chosen to maintain the pretence of an outwardly cordial relationship for the sake of appearances while harbouring intense feelings of hostility towards each other.

Where the murder may be the culmination of a dispute of some sort, the family liaison officer should be looking for information about any falling out between friends or acquaintances, unexplained injuries that the victim may have had, criminal damage to motor vehicle, strange phone calls, financial disputes or a marked change in the behaviour of the victim that may be linked to a chain of events. Investigators should also be mindful that if an event can be identified then the potential for forensic opportunities should not be overlooked.

Case study

When Janet Marshall was murdered in her own home in Tottenham on 30 April 1991, an initial investigation pointed to the possibility that her husband might have been involved, because there seemed to have been no forced entry into the home. A second investigation, however, uncovered the fact that in the years leading up to Janet's murder the family had received a number of poison pen letters. On one occasion one of the letters mentioned important information about the inside of the home. The content of the letters was designed to drive a wedge between the married couple. These letters had been reported to the police but unfortunately the letter writer was never traced.

When interviewed by the second enquiry team Mr Marshall, who worked as a driving instructor, alluded to a female pupil, Rene Sampat, who had become obsessed with him while taking driving lessons some years before. He had immediately stopped giving her lessons but she then joined the church where the Marshall family worshipped. Since it was the custom of the Baptist Church to receive and welcome fellow members of the congregation into one's home after worship, Sampat had found her way into the Marshall family home after church services.

During this period a set of keys went missing from the Marshall's kitchen, only to turn up again shortly afterwards. The Marshall's thought that this was because their children had misplaced them.

Rene Sampat and her son, Roy Aziz, were convicted of Janet's murder in February 2004 after a second investigation into her death. Much of the evidence against them was achieved through the careful collection of victimology, with special attention being paid to significant precursor events. The letters that had been sent to the Marshall family over a year before Janet's death had Sampat's fingerprints and DNA on them.

It transpired that Sampat had taken keys from the family home after church. She had copied them and replaced them on a later occasion. On the night of Janet's murder her son had entered the premises using a key and stabbed Janet to death. Roy Aziz had been persuaded to do this by his mother with the ultimate aim being that she could have the man that she obsessed with after Janet was gone. Sampat was sentenced to life imprisonment and her son was detained at Her Majesty's Pleasure.

5.5.2 **Finances**

Looking at a victim's financial position can often be beneficial in developing victimology. The fact that someone is in debt to another individual is clearly going to be of interest to an investigation. Beyond that, however, some analysis of how they spend their money may lead an investigation into areas of interest. For instance, if someone is living way beyond their means there is potential that they are indebted to someone financially. Another way of looking at a victim's lifestyle through their financial transactions is by examining the purchases they have made using credit/debit/store cards. If they have been purchasing gifts for a romantic partner or staying in hotels that no one close to them knows about it could mean that there is a part of their life that is hidden. These areas need to be explored.

KEY POINT - FINANCES

Finances include all sources of income (legitimate and otherwise), all outgoings, savings, loans and any other debts including credit cards, store cards, hire-purchase agreements, loans from family, friends and unlicensed lenders, and anything else involving the transaction of money (eg gambling habits).

5.5.3 Lifestyle

How does the victim live his or her life? An old adage that is often quoted in law enforcement circles is, 'if you find out how someone lived, you will find out how they died'.

Lifestyle enquires may include whether people have a job, who they work with, where they work, the nature of their business when they are between jobs, when and how they collect any benefit payments, their hobbies or any sporting or other activities that they take part in, how often they participate in these activities, where they participate in these activities, their role in these activities and who they come into contact with when they participate in these activities. The purpose of lifestyle enquiries of this nature is to establish where the victim may have previously come into contact with their killer. By developing their lifestyle profile more can be learnt about the victim.

KEY POINT - VICTIMOLOGY AND MOTIVES FOR MURDER

It is important to make enquiries into the deceased's lifestyle, such as their job and place of work, their hobbies and who they came into contact with, as this may establish any possible motives for murder.

Lifestyle enquiries can focus on potential motives for homicide, as well as on people who may have had the opportunity to commit the crime by virtue of being in contact with the victim. This is certainly true when people with 'high-risk' lifestyles are considered. Do they take or deal in drugs, are they a heavy drinker, are they involved in prostitution, do they move in criminal circles, are they a heavy gambler etc.? All these are difficult questions to ask a family when they have just lost a loved one. The competence and experience of the family liaison officer is very important here. If lifestyle is an issue it is important to explain to the family why at such a terrible time the police need to ask difficult questions of this nature. In the absence of such an explanation the family may not understand why the police are pursuing these lines of enquiry and conclude that the police are needlessly spending too much time trying to find out negative information about their loved one as opposed to trying to find out who killed them. It is important that the police are not judgmental when pursuing this type of information.

5.5.4 **Behaviour**

An exploration of the deceased's behaviour centres on the question 'what sort of person were they?' Were they happy, fun, depressed, worried, preoccupied, anxious, aggressive, laid back, secretive etc.? In what circumstances might they have displayed this type of behaviour? Did they move from one type of behaviour to another and, if they did, what triggered the mood change? Had their personality changed recently? What were the circumstances? How might they have reacted in certain circumstances—would they have stood their ground, fought or run away from trouble? Were they likely to start trouble? Did they drink alcohol or take drugs and, if so, did their character change when they had been drinking or taking drugs? An exploration of such behaviour may contribute toward an understanding of the circumstances in which the victim died.

5.5.5 **Geography**

An exploration of the victim's geography focuses on their movements, both on a day-to-day basis and over the course of their lifetime. This means that the family liaison officer may ask questions about the person's background, such as 'how long had they been living here?' and 'where did they come from?'. They may also ask questions like 'where did the victim move around (eg home to workplace, workplace to leisure)? How did they travel? What routes did they take? This information is important when trying to locate sightings or possible CCTV opportunities.

It is important that the family liaison officer does not make assumptions about routes. A good interviewer should illicit all the pertinent details from the witness using proper interview techniques and this includes considering whether there is a relationship between the victim's geography and the crime scene. For example, could it be that the victim passed the scene on route elsewhere (eg home, work or elsewhere for leisure)?

Geography is not confined to that surrounding the deceased. Having established a full list of friends and associates of the deceased, questions also need to be asked intended to establish whether anyone within the victim's circle of acquaintances has a relationship either with the scene or the area surrounding the scene.

By gathering in-depth geographical data about the victim the family liaison officer can help those leading the investigation to prioritize lines of enquiry that focus on people who had the geographic opportunity to kill the deceased.

5.5.6 **Associates: work and play**

Given that the statistics indicate the killer may be an acquaintance it is important to establish who knew most about the deceased. The killer may well come from within this category. It is, therefore, the case that a massive amount of detail is required when interviewing the family about this area.

All known associates are crucial, including people who attend the family home during the family liaison officer's deployment. It is crucial that the family liaison officer keeps accurate records about the people that they come into contact with in the family home. This is essential for maintaining an accurate and up-to-date risk assessment of the continuing deployment. It also helps to understand the victim and their relationship with those who knew most about them.

It may also be useful for the family liaison officer to ask the family whether they can think of anybody who has not been in touch with them from whom they would have expected contact in the circumstances.

Records of associates need to be created and personal descriptive forms completed. If they are not created they do not exist; if they do not exist they cannot be interviewed or researched.

5.5.7 **Friends and family**

Who are the family? The definition set out by the Association of Chief Police Officers (ACPO) as reported in chapter 2 is wide for a reason. A family tree is a very useful tool for investigators. This is not necessarily because the suspect lies within this area but because the best place to build up knowledge about the victim probably starts here.

Finding out who was the closest to the deceased is not just about blood relationships. A useful way of approaching this is to think about our own lives. Who knows your innermost thoughts and opinions? It is not always the next-of-kin or the closest relative. They can, however, help the investigation to identify and locate other people who can help build up the fullest possible picture of the victim's life. If the family liaison officer feeds information about those closest to the victim outside the family back into the investigation as soon as possible, someone can be tasked to go and speak to them as a matter of urgency.

Family liaison officers also need to be effective investigators because they need to be able to pick up important, non-verbal communications between family members and friends. There are many reasons why a grieving family may want to paint a slightly inaccurate picture of their loved one's memory. This is natural for grieving people. The family liaison officer needs to be able to coax information from families to assist the investigation. Sometimes the family liaison officer needs the type of information that the families at this terrible time would rather not talk about. This is a complex time in the relationship between police and family. Given the complexity and scale of this task it is extremely doubtful that it can be achieved effectively and efficiently by a single family liaison officer deployment.

5.5.8 **Routine: work and play**

It is important to stress that the areas in the 'victimology' model are deliberately not in any order, although to achieve the answers to the whole model the family liaison officer will need to develop a picture of family, friends and associates. They should then be in a position to examine the other areas. For example, establishing a picture of the deceased's family and associates in conjunction with their everyday geographic routine is likely to shed some light on the various points at which different people come into contact with the victim. This is important because when victim, suspect and scene are considered in the context of a homicide enquiry investigators usually ask what brought these three things together in such lethal circumstances.

5.6 **Chapter Summary**

As with most other types of crime, the three variables that come together in any homicide are scene, suspect and victim. Victimology is intended to shed some light on why these variables came together when they did with such terrible consequences.

Identifying why someone has died in a criminal act can sometimes be a vague and subjective exercise. That is why the police service employs analysts, behavioural and geographical advisers. While it is not the role of the family liaison officer to analyse the information that they gather from the family to any great extent it is hard to see how these other areas of investigative expertise can operate effectively without their contribution. It is important to understand that while family liaison officers are often the cornerstone of any victimology strategy, their work is the start of a process; it is not an end in itself. Family liaison officers make an important and often vital contribution to an investigation by building the foundations for what is to follow; they need to do this as a matter of urgency under effective supervision and management. The work of the family liaison officer should always be driven by the senior investigating officer's family liaison strategy.

NOTES

6

Witness Assessment and Interviewing

6.1 Introduction

This chapter sets out to look at the role of the family liaison officer in terms of an initial witness assessment and its contribution to the interview planning process.

Witness assessment has increasingly become part of the family liaison officers' role. It largely consists of recognizing that someone is a witness, categorizing the witness into one or more predetermined group, and the provisional prioritization of the witness in terms of the likely importance of their information to the investigation and availability for interview.

Family liaison officers are, however, unlikely to conduct the witness interview because they tend to have rather more knowledge of the investigation than is desirable for a witness interviewer and because they may need to ask challenging or intimate questions of the witness that might result in the nature of their relationship with the family being needlessly compromised.

Once they have played their part in witness assessment, however, the family liaison officers' job is far from done. The knowledge that they have of the witness is a vital component of the planning process and the contribution that they can make to the preparation of the witness for the interview could be invaluable.

6.2 Witness Categorization

As family liaison officers begin to interact with the family one of their first priorities must be to identify any witnesses within the family because the investigation team will not necessarily know who they are in advance of the deployment of a family liaison officer.

What then is a witness? The answer to this question may seem a little obvious at first glance but it is an answer that underpins decisions about who should interview individuals within the family and how to record the information they provide. Quite simply a witness is someone who might to be called to give evidence in court (see, for example, s 63 Youth Justice and Criminal Evidence Act 1999, s 52 Domestic Violence, Crime and Victims Act 2004 and para 5.8 of the Code of Practice for Victims of Crime (Office for Criminal Justice Reform, 2005)).

KEY POINT – DEFINITION OF A WITNESS

A witness is someone who might to be called to give evidence in court.

It is, therefore, the case that a witness is someone who might give evidence because they have seen or heard something of the events during which a death took place or events closely related to it (for example, a threat, incriminating comments made by a suspected offender, the ownership or disposal of weapons or other property connected to a death). In addition to this, members of the family who are in a position to provide an alibi to a known suspect should also be treated as witnesses, because the alibi might subsequently feature in criminal proceedings either to refute an allegation from the defence to the effect that the person to whom the alibi applies, rather than their client, committed the offence or in support of the prosecution of the person to whom the alibi applies, and indeed the witness, in the event of it turning out to be a deliberate falsehood.

While the background material that makes up a victimology (see chapter 5) will often be crucial to the successful conclusion of an investigation, it is not usually the stuff of evidence. It follows that, in most investigations, while most members of the family can contribute toward a victimology, few of them will be witnesses. That having been said, the family liaison officer is often best placed to identify previously unknown witnesses in the family.

6.3 Initial Contact with Witnesses

When encountering for the first time in the family a potential witness to an offence there is a tension between needing to ask them some questions to find out what they know while trying to minimize the scope for future challenges that allege the witness's memory was corrupted in some way by the initial contact.

The 'rules' set out in *Achieving Best Evidence in Criminal Proceedings: Guidance on Interviewing Victims and Witnesses, and Using Special Measures* (Office for Criminal Justice Reform, 2007) take account of this tension in that they acknowledge the need for some questioning to take place to determine the initial action that is to be taken by the police while seeking to limit the questions to those that are necessary for early decision-making. These rules can be summarized as follows:

- Listen: do not interrupt unsolicited accounts.
- Try to ask open and specific-closed questions; try to avoid less productive types of question.
- Only ask what is necessary to determine initial action (this depends on the circumstances).
- Make a written record of what was said, who was present and the witness's demeanour as soon as possible.

6.4 Witness Categorization

Having identified a member of the family as a witness the next step will be for the family liaison officer to conduct a preliminary assessment to place the witness in one or more of the predetermined categories. In England and Wales, there are currently four categories of witness:

1) vulnerable;
2) intimidated;
3) significant;
4) other.

Section 137 Criminal Justice Act 2003 will introduce another category when it is implemented. Section 137 is briefly mentioned in 'significant' witnesses below.

6.4.1 Vulnerable witnesses

'Vulnerable' witnesses are defined by s 16 of the Youth Justice and Criminal Evidence Act 1999 as:

- children under 17 (under 18 when s 98 of the Coroners and Justice Act 2009 is implemented); and
- people whose quality of evidence is likely to be diminished because they:
  - are suffering from a mental disorder (as defined by the Mental Health Act 1983, as amended by the Mental Health Act 2007); or
  - have a significant impairment of intelligence and social functioning; or
  - have a physical disability or are suffering from a physical disorder.

At the time of writing the first group of witnesses in this category, children under 17, were also regarded as 'in need of special protection' under s 21 of the Youth Justice and Criminal Evidence Act 1999 in the case of sexual or violent offences. Violent offences include 'any offence ... which involves an assault on, or injury or a threat of injury to, any person' and, therefore, the kind of offences to which a family liaison officer would usually be deployed (ie murder, manslaughter, road death). The importance of being 'in need of special protection' is that there is a stronger presupposition that these child witnesses will give their evidence-in-chief by prerecorded video and that they will be cross-examined via live television link. Section 100 of the Coroners and Justice Act 2009 will, however, abolish the category of children in need of special protection and introduce a provision whereby the child can 'opt' out of video-recorded evidence-in-chief if they wish to do so when it is implemented. In circumstances where the child exercises the right to opt out it is assumed that they will give all their evidence by means of live television link or screens unless they also wish to opt out of these special measures. Investigative interviews with child witnesses within the family should, therefore, usually be video-recorded with a view to playing them as evidence-in-chief unless the child or their parents/guardian refuses consent.

The second group of witnesses in this category is adults whose quality of evidence is likely to be diminished by virtue of a mental disorder, learning disability, or a physical disorder or disability. The disability may be either lifelong (for example, a learning disability) or acquired (for example, dementia). Quality of evidence for these purposes refers to its 'completeness, coherence and accuracy' (s 16(5) of the Youth Justice and Criminal Evidence Act 1999). In essence, this means that the disorder or disability must have an adverse impact on the ability of the witness to communicate to such an extent that it is likely to affect their evidence. The effect of this is that not all witnesses with a disability will be regarded as 'vulnerable'. For example, a witness who has a severe visual impairment would only be regarded as 'vulnerable' if their inability to see could have an adverse impact on their ability to communicate with others.

Example – vulnerable adult witness

A wheel chair user would only be regarded as 'vulnerable' for the purposes of s 16 Youth Justice and Criminal Evidence Act 1999 if their ability to communicate is impaired by the condition that makes the use of a wheel chair necessary or they have another condition that has an adverse impact on their ability to communicate. The key issue here is that the disorder or the disability must have an adverse impact on the witness's ability to communicate. In cases where the witness has a disability that does not have an impact on their ability to communicate they would not be regarded as 'vulnerable' for the purposes of the 'special measures' set out in the Youth Justice and Criminal Evidence Act 1999, even though disability discrimination legislation regarding access to the court etc. still applies.

6.4.2 Intimidated witnesses

'Intimidated' witnesses are defined by s 17 of the Youth Justice and Criminal Evidence Act 1999 as those whose quality of evidence is likely to be diminished by reason of fear or distress in connection with testifying at court. As in the case of vulnerable adult witnesses, quality of evidence refers to its 'completeness, coherence and accuracy', so the fear or distress must be so great as to be likely to have an impact on the witness's ability to communicate in court.

Section 17(2) of the Youth Justice and Criminal Evidence Act 1999 goes on to say that the court should take account of the following when determining whether a witness falls into this category:

- the nature and alleged circumstances of the offence;
- the age of the witness;
- where relevant:
  - the social and cultural background and ethnic origins of the witness;
  - the domestic and employment circumstances of the witness; and
  - any religious beliefs or political opinions of the witness;

- any behaviour toward the witness by:
  - the accused;
  - members of the accused person's family or associates;
  - any other person who is likely to be either an accused person or a witness in the proceedings.

Complainants to sexual offences are defined as falling into this category per se by s 17(4) of the Youth Justice and Criminal Evidence Act 1999. Section 99 of the Coroners and Justice Act 2009 will make similar provisions for witnesses to certain gun and knife crimes by inserting a new s 17(5) into the Youth Justice and Criminal Evidence Act 1999 when it is implemented.

Vulnerable Witnesses: A Police Service Guide (Home Office, 2002) and *Achieving Best Evidence in Criminal Proceedings: Guidance on Interviewing Victims and Witnesses, and Using Special Measures* (Office for Criminal Justice Reform, 2007) suggest that victims of domestic abuse, racially motivated crime and repeat victimization and witnesses who self-neglect/self-harm or who are elderly and frail, also fall into this category. The *Code of Practice for Victims of Crime* (Office for Criminal Justice Reform, 2005) extends this when it recommends that 'the relatives of those who have died as a result of criminal conduct should also be regarded as 'intimidated' within the meaning of s 17. It is, therefore, the case that witnesses from the families of murder, manslaughter or road death victims are 'intimidated' and that they are eligible for special measures in court such as screens, live television link and video–recorded evidence-in-chief if they are likely to maximize the quality of their evidence.

6.4.2.1 **Special measures**

Subject to availability, as defined in a phased implementation timetable, vulnerable and intimidated witnesses may be eligible for the following 'special measures' under Part 2 of the Youth Justice and Criminal Evidence Act 1999:

- the use of screens (s 23);
- the use of live TV link (s 24);
- giving evidence in private (s 25);
- the removal of wigs and gowns (s 26);
- the use of video-recorded interviews as evidence-in-chief (s 27);
- communication through intermediaries (s 29); and
- the use of special communication aids (s 30).

The use of video-recorded cross-examination is also listed as a special measure under s 28 Youth Justice and Criminal Evidence Act 1999, but this had not been implemented at the time of writing.

6.4.2.2 **Screens**

Screens or curtains (depending on the layout of the court) are positioned around the witness box so as to prevent the defendant from seeing the witness and the witness from seeing the defendant. The witness will still be able to see and be seen by the judge or magistrate, at least one legal representative of the prosecution and defence (and the jury if the case is heard at the Crown Court). This special measure is available for all vulnerable and intimidated witnesses in all criminal courts in England and Wales.

6.4.2.3 **Live TV link**

The witness gives live evidence from a room outside the courtroom (usually, though not always, in the court building). The witness's testimony is relayed live into the courtroom via TV link. This measure is intended to reduce the stress experienced by witnesses while they give evidence by taking them out of the intimidating auditorium of the courtroom and out of the presence of the accused, although it should be noted that the accused will be able to see the witness on the television screen unless additional provisions are made to preserve their anonymity. This special measure is available for all vulnerable and intimidated witnesses in all criminal courts in England and Wales. Section 102 of the Coroners and Justice Act 2009 will insert a new sub-section into s 24 of the Youth Justice and Criminal Evidence Act 1999 (s 24(1A) and (1B)), when it is implemented, providing for a nominated witness supporter to be present in the live television link room.

6.4.2.4 **Giving evidence in private**

Members of the public are excluded from the court while the witness is giving evidence. Only one nominated member of the media is allowed to be present. This measure is only available in sexual offences and in some cases of intimidation. It is intended to reduce the embarrassment and/or sense of intimidation likely to be experienced while witnesses give sensitive evidence. This special measure is available for all vulnerable and intimidated witnesses in all criminal courts in England and Wales.

6.4.2.5 **The removal of wigs and gowns**

The judge and lawyers remove their wigs and gowns with the intention of creating a less formal environment in the court leading to a reduction in the anxiety experienced by the witness. This measure is only of use where the witness does not prefer the formality of the situation to be enhanced by wigs and gowns. Some witnesses might express the view that they want 'their day in a *proper* court'. This special measure is available for all vulnerable and intimidated witnesses in all criminal courts in England and Wales.

6.4.2.6 **The use of video-recorded interviews as evidence-in-chief**

The video interview with the police (with social services present in appropriate cases) is played as the witness's evidence-in-chief with the intention of reducing the stress experienced by the witness as a result of reducing the number of times on which they have to repeat their account. It is important to remember that the witness must be available to attend court to give evidence (s 27(4) Youth Justice and Criminal Evidence Act 1999), although cross-examination often takes place via live TV link in these circumstances.

A video-recorded interview can only be played in court where the witness is not available for cross-examination in the wholly exceptional circumstances set out in the hearsay provisions described in s 116 of the Criminal Justice Act 2003. These exceptions are:

- where the witness is dead;
- where the witness is physically or mentally unfit to give evidence;
- where the witness is outside the UK and it has not been practical to secure their attendance in court;
- where the witness cannot be found even though all reasonable steps have been taken to find them;
- where the witness cannot give evidence through fear.

For the purposes of s 116 of the Criminal Justice Act 2003, 'fear' includes fear of the death or injury of another person or of financial loss. In these circumstances, however, the court can only admit a statement made by the witness in their absence if they consider it is in the interests of justice to do so.

Video-recorded interviews are served on the defence as part of the prosecution case where they are to be played as evidence-in-chief. The visual image can only be pixilated and the voice recording can only be modulated where an application is made for witness anonymity under s 87 of the Coroners and Justice Act 2009.

The Appeal Court judgment in the case of *R v Rochester* [2008] EWCA Crim 678 overturned previous views concerning the phased implementation of this special measure. It has been available to all vulnerable and intimidated witness in all the criminal courts in England and Wales since 24 July 2002.

6.4.2.7 **The use of video-recorded cross-examination**

Cross-examination is video-recorded before the trial and played at the trial. This special measure was originally intended to reduce the stress experienced by witnesses as a result of cross-examination having been completed before the trial. It has, however, run into some practical difficulties that include the continuing duty of disclosure by the prosecution to the defence. The prosecution have a continuing duty of disclosure to the defence by virtue of the Criminal Procedure and Investigations Act 1996 (as amended by s 37 of the Criminal Justice Act 2003). The effect of this is that the witness might still be called to court if fresh information comes to light after video-recorded cross-examination. This special measure had not been implemented at the time of writing as a result of these practical difficulties.

6.4.2.8 Communication through intermediaries

The function of an intermediary is to assist 'vulnerable' witnesses (as defined by s 16 of the Youth Justice and Criminal Evidence Act 1999) to communicate by *explaining* questions put to and answers given by them. This special measure is for witnesses who would benefit from the assistance of a specialist, such as a speech and language therapist, a clinical psychologist, a mental health professional or a special needs education professional, to help them to communicate in a police witness interview and/or while giving evidence during legal proceedings. At the time of writing the intermediary matching service could be contacted at the Specialist Operations Centre of the National Policing Improvement Agency. This special measure is available for all vulnerable witnesses in all criminal courts in England and Wales.

6.4.2.9 The use of special communication aids

This special measure is intended to help 'vulnerable' witnesses who need to use a 'device' to communicate when giving evidence. This includes computers and voice synthesizers; it might also include symbol boards and books. This special measure is available to vulnerable witnesses in all criminal courts in England and Wales.

6.4.2.10 Eligibility for special measures

When a witness is considered to fall into either the 'vulnerable' or 'intimidated' category they are deemed to be 'eligible' for 'special measures'. However, whether or not they are actually given access to such measures by the court depends on two considerations:

1) whether the 'special measure' in question has been implemented; and
2) with the exception of live TV link and video-recorded evidence-in-chief in respect of child witnesses 'in need of special protection', whether the 'special measure' in question is likely to maximize the quality of their evidence (s 19(2)).

In determining whether the quality of the witness's evidence is likely to be maximized, courts are obliged to take account of the circumstances of the case, including witness's views and the likelihood that the use of the 'special measure' might inhibit the testing of the evidence by any party (s 19(3)). It follows that investigators should ensure that the informed views of 'vulnerable' or 'intimidated' witnesses are sought in relation to those 'special measures' that are currently available to them. Explaining special measures to victims is a police responsibility under the *Code of Practice for Victims of Crime* (para 5.8) (Office for Criminal Justice Reform, 2005) and the *Witness Charter,* charter standards 4 and 5 (Office for Criminal Justice Reform, 2007). Investigators involved in soliciting the views of 'vulnerable' or 'intimidated' witnesses should make it clear to them that the final decision concerning access to special measures is a matter for the court.

In addition, the availability of the special measure and the likelihood that it will maximize the quality of the witness's evidence, access to video-recorded evidence-in-chief is also contingent on whether playing the video or any part of it is contrary to the interests of justice (s 27(2)).

6.4.3 **Significant witnesses**

Significant witnesses are defined by *Achieving Best Evidence in Criminal Proceedings: Guidance on Interviewing Victims and Witnesses* and *Using Special Measures* (Office for Criminal Justice Reform, 2007) as those who:

- have or claim to have witnessed, visually or otherwise, an indictable offence, part of such an offence or events closely connected with it;
- stand in a particular relationship to the victim or have a central position in an investigation into an indictable offence.

There is currently no statutory provision in England and Wales for video-recorded interviews with significant witnesses to be played as evidence-in-chief. It is, however, generally considered good practice to record interviews with significant witnesses in this way because a video provides a highly accurate and transparent record of what was said. For this reason, a video-recording is a more effective means of rebutting challenges to the integrity of the interview than in the case of written notes alone. Audio-recording could be used as an alternative because it also provides a more complete record of what was said than notes, although it misses the visual context.

There are two ways in which the material on a video-recorded interview with a significant witness may be used as evidence:

1) The witness makes a brief written statement that effectively adopts what was said in the interview as soon afterwards as possible. Such a statement should not go into any detail but would usually be limited to something like 'on *day, date, time* and *place* I was at my home address with my brother, [*name*], when somebody wearing a mask broke down the door and shot him with a gun. I was subsequently interviewed on video by DC Bloggs at [*place*] about this. What I told the officer was true to the best of my recollection.' A transcript should then be compiled and produced by the interviewer as an exhibit while the recording is usually disclosed to the defence as unused material in compliance with the Criminal Procedure and Investigations Act 1996.
2) Following the interview and in the absence of the witness, the interviewer prepares a full written statement from the recording. The witness is then asked to review and sign the statement. The video is disclosed to the defence as unused material.

The second of these options is considered the preferred method because the preparation of a transcript has more resource implications for everybody in the criminal justice system, although it is accepted that it may be necessary to make use of the first of these options in circumstances where the witness's subsequent availability to sign a full written statement is in doubt (eg as a result of going away on a lengthy holiday or a change of mind coming about due to fear of the consequences.

Some witnesses who are currently categorized as 'significant' will eventually be eligible for video-recorded evidence-in-chief, when s 137 of the Criminal Justice Act 2003 is implemented in England and Wales. Section 137 applies to witnesses 'who have or claim to have witnessed, visually or otherwise, an indictable or prescribed triable either way offence, part of such an offence, or events closely connected with it' in circumstances where the interview takes place so soon after the event that the witness's recollection is likely to be significantly better at the time of the interview than at the time of giving evidence.

6.4.4 Other witnesses

'Other' witnesses are simply those who do not fall into the vulnerable, intimidated or significant categories.

6.5 Witness Prioritization

In any large major investigation the number of witnesses to be interviewed will usually exceed the resources, in terms of interviewers, facilities and equipment that are available to conduct the interviews. In these circumstances any witness interview strategy will need to include a mechanism for prioritizing the interviews. Prioritization consists simply of determining the order in which the witnesses are to be interviewed. Two methods are generally used to prioritize witness interviews:

1) As they are identified, witnesses are referred to the officer in charge of the investigation or nominee (for example an interview adviser) to assess the likely importance of their account to the investigation on the basis of what they have already told the police, what other witnesses have said, CCTV footage, relationship to suspect etc.
2) Where there are multiple witnesses who need to be interviewed urgently, a number of parameters pre-specified by the officer in charge of the investigation are applied (for example, proximity to the incident, and line of sight).

The information obtained by family liaison officers following initial contact with a witness in the family can provide a crucial basis for decision-making in respect of the prioritization of the interview with that witness.

6.6 Interview Planning

6.6.1 Consent to interview

Witness interviews should take place with the informed consent of the interviewee. 'Informed consent' in this context refers to understanding the purpose of the interview (eg to be played as evidence-in-chief or, in the case of a written statement, to help the prosecution lawyer guide the witness through live evidence-in-chief). Informed consent is not only a moral imperative it is also a procedural requirement that arises from the *Code of Practice for Victims of Crime* (Office for Criminal Justice Reform, 2005) and the *Witness Charter* (Office for Criminal Justice Reform, 2007).

Where the witness is under 17, consideration needs to be given to the guidelines specified by Lord Fraser in the case involving Victoria Gillick in 1985 (*Gillick v West Norfolk and Wisbech AHA* [1985] 3 All ER 402). The effect of the Fraser guidelines is that a child can consent in their own right if they are capable of understanding the implications of what they are being asked to consent to. If a child can understand the implications of being interviewed as a witness and, where the interview is to be video-recorded, the use to which the recording is to be put, they can consent in their own right. If a child cannot understand these implications, the consent of a parent or guardian is required. *Achieving Best Evidence* recommends that the child's parents/guardians should be informed, even where a child has the capacity to consent, other than in wholly exceptional circumstances.

The Mental Capacity Act 2005 applies where the witness is over 16 and there is some doubt whether they have the mental capacity to understand the implications of what they are being asked to consent to (for example where a witness has a severe learning disability). The Act puts an obligation on service providers such as the police to try their utmost to communicate with people for whom capacity may be an issue. The effect of this is that the language used to communicate the information on which a decision is to be based may need to be modified. Where it is determined that a witness still lacks the capacity to make an informed decision, the police are required to act in the person's 'best interests'. Acting in a person's 'best interests' means consulting every available person who is involved in the witness's life about what the witness would want if they had the capacity to make a decision.

6.6.2 Planning and preparation

Planning for an interview consists of obtaining information about the witness and then using it in conjunction with what is known about the offence and the investigation to make various decisions about the conduct of the interview. The family liaison officer's knowledge and experience of the family is likely to be such that it can make a crucial contribution to this process, even where they are not involved in the interview itself.

6.6.2.1 The witness

The information about the witness that should be established for the purposes of planning the interview includes:

- age;
- gender;
- sexuality (if relevant to the offence and likely to have an impact on the interview, eg in terms of interviewer selection);
- culture, ethnicity, religion and first language;
- preferred name/mode of address;
- domestic circumstances (including whether currently in a 'safe' environment);
- the implications of any physical, learning or mental disorder or disability for the interview process;
- the implications of any medication taken for the interview process;
- current emotional state (including trauma, distress, shock, depression, fears of intimidation/recrimination and recent significant stressful events experienced);
- likely impact of recalling of traumatic events on the behaviour of the witness;
- current or previous contact with public services (including previous contact with police, social services or health professionals);
- relationship to the alleged offender.

6.6.2.2 The offence

As noted in the introduction to this chapter, in ideal situations interviewers should only have minimal offence information because of the potential that such knowledge has to contaminate the interview. Such minimal offence information includes:

- the nature of the alleged offence;
- the time, frequency and location of the alleged offence;
- how the alleged offence came to the notice of police;
- the nature of any threats or intimidation alleged to have been used by the suspect of their associates.

Family liaison officers are likely to know far more about the offence than this limited information and should not usually serve as interviewers as a result. Where, however, it is thought that the potential disadvantages of the family liaison officer's knowledge of the offence are outweighed by other issues such as the rapport that they have established with the witness and they have been appropriately trained it may be considered desirable that they should conduct the interview. In these circumstances, it is essential that family liaison officers do their best to guard against their knowledge of the case contaminating the interview.

6.6.2.3 Information important to the investigation

Information important to the investigation can be thought of as falling into two categories:

1) matters of general investigative practice;
2) case-specific material.

Matters of general investigative practice include:

- points to prove the offence;
- case law (for example, *R v Turnbull* [1977] QB 224 in the case of eye-witnesses);
- good investigative practice (for example, 'have you told anyone else about this?').

As is suggested in the name, case-specific material very much depends on the particular circumstances of the case. It could include:

- the witness's knowledge about various aspects of the victim or suspect's antecedents;
- the background to the relationship between a victim and a suspect;
- a history of the alleged abuse experienced by a victim or a suspect;
- the victim or suspect's usual routine;
- the victim or suspect's ownership, control or use of property such as vehicles, mobile telephones and computers;
- the suspect's access to weapons;
- the victim or suspect's access to a crime scene;
- the suspect's access to material that could be used to conceal or cleanse a crime scene.

Matters of general investigative practice are invariably of evidential value; case-specific material usually has little or no evidential value, even though it often proves crucial in the successful resolution of an investigation. The principal function of case-specific material is to aid the investigative process by contributing to the investigation team's understanding of the alleged offence and by generating lines of enquiry.

Interviewers should know a great deal about matters of general investigative practice when they prepare for interview. The amount of case-specific material that they have access to before the interview usually depends on how much they know about the alleged offence. The interview plan will need to take account of situations in which interviewers have no knowledge of some or all the case-specific material. In these circumstances the case-specific material might be handled either by being 'drip-fed' to the interviewers at a suitable point in the interview by someone monitoring the process or, where the case is complex, by the interview taking place in two parts separated by a break during which the interviewers can be briefed on the case-specific material.

6.6.2.4 **Use of planning information**

The planning information should then be used to determine the following:

- the objectives of the interview;
- the most appropriate structure for the interview;
- the techniques to be used during the interview;
- the method of recording the interview;
- any props and exhibits that should be available to the interviewers;
- the people to be present during the interview:
  - interviewers (if two, who will lead?)
  - camera operator
  - interview monitor (if appropriate)
  - witness supporter (if requested by the witness)
  - interpreter (if necessary)
  - intermediary (if necessary);
- the timing of the interview;
- the likely duration and pace of the interview
- whether more than one interview session is likely to be needed.

6.6.3 **Objectives**

The objectives for any interview should be clear, topic-based and specific. General objectives such as 'to find out what the witness knows about the offence' are of little use in determining the ground to be covered during the interview. The objectives should clearly identify the incident-related topics (for example, the witness's movements between particular times) and the case-specific information important to the investigation that the interview should focus on (for example, the various vehicles that a known suspect has access to).

6.6.4 **Interview structure**

The most appropriate framework for an investigative interview is usually the four-phased structure described in *Achieving Best Evidence*. There are, however, occasions on which the phased approach is unlikely to be of any use such as where the witness has very limited communication ability (particularly where they can only indicate 'yes' or 'no' in response to a question). In these circumstances a decision will need to be made on an alternative structure for the interview, eg a series of carefully framed forced-choice questions.

6.6.5 **Interview techniques**

The techniques to be used during the interview could include:

- the cognitive interview (see chapter 4B of *Achieving Best Evidence*) where the witness is either an eye- or an ear-witness to an event and is willing and able

to focus their concentration to the extent needed mentally to reinstate the context;
- conversation management (see *Practical Guide to Investigative Interviewing* (Association of Chief Police Officers, 2004)) where the witness is unable or unwilling to focus their concentration or where their account does not deal with a specific incident (for example, where background material is to be covered in the interview).

The techniques chosen for any particular phase of the interview very much depend on what the interviewer knows about the witness and what they are trying to achieve, as specified in the objectives for the interview. It may be, for example, that an interviewer will choose to use the cognitive technique of mentally reinstating the context of the to-be-remembered event when trying to initiate a free-narrative account. It is beyond the scope of this chapter and indeed this book to describe every technique in the cognitive interview or the substantial body of research that underpins it; suffice to say that mentally reinstating the context is a technique that involves encouraging the witness to reconstruct the physical and mental context of an event as they experienced it. The use of this technique can be entirely appropriate and extremely effective in terms of enhancing recall in the right circumstances. Those circumstances are that the recall sought must relate to a specified event and that the witness must be willing and able to commit the mental resources needed to concentrate and focus on their memory of the event mentally to reinstate the context. The technique cannot be used if the memory sought relates to general biographical or conceptual information (eg the history and background to a relationship, ownership or use of vehicles or digital technology). It also cannot be used if the witness is reluctant in any way or if their mental condition is such that concentrating and focusing on their memory of a specific event is not a realistic option (eg a witness who is severely clinically depressed is unlikely to be able to concentrate to the extent required to mentally reinstate the context). Where mentally reinstating the context is inappropriate, alternative techniques should be used. For example, where a witness cannot mentally reinstate the context due to their mental condition, simply saying 'tell me what happened' is likely to be the most effective way of initiating a free-narrative account.

Reference should be made to *Achieving Best Evidence* or any one of the many good books about interviewing for more information on interview techniques.

6.6.6 **Method of recording**

When interviews with vulnerable and intimidated witnesses are recorded with a view to playing them as evidence-in-chief the recording must be on video because s 27 of the Youth Justice and Criminal Evidence Act only provides for the playing of a video-recording (no provision is made for audio-recordings). It is important, however, to remember that it is the informed views of the witness that determine whether a video is actually made. Where a witness does not want the interview to be video-recorded consideration can be given to making an audio-recording if the witness is also 'significant'. If the witness does not want the interview to be audio-recorded or they are not considered 'significant' a record of the interview should be made in the form of handwritten notes.

Interviews with significant witnesses should usually be recorded on video since this medium is likely to provide the most comprehensive record of the interview. If the witness does not want the interview to be video-recorded consideration should be given to making an audio record of it. If the witness does not want the interview to be audio-recorded, handwritten notes should suffice (*Achieving Best Evidence,* paras 4.53–4.54).

6.6.7 **Location**

Video-recorded interviews should ideally take place in purpose-built interview suites; they are designed to keep background noise and visual distractions to a minimum. Portable video-recording equipment should only be used where it is not practical to access a purpose-built suite.

6.6.8 **Props and exhibits**

Props and exhibits might include:

- pens and paper;
- body diagrams;
- property;
- photographs.

It can be helpful to have pens and paper in the interview room but body diagrams, property and photographs have the potential to distract and, possibly, lead a witness. For this reason they should be kept out of sight, possibly in the room with the camera operator, and only brought out when they are needed in the interview. If the witness writes or draws on any paper in the interview it should be treated as an exhibit.

6.6.9 **People present**

A camera operator should always be present when the interview is video-recorded. In addition to this, the circumstances of the witness and the case may merit the presence of the following:

- a second interviewer and/or interview monitor;
- a witness supporter;
- an interpreter;
- an intermediary.

Where a second interviewer is to be present there should be a clear agreement as to who will lead the interview and an understanding of how and when the second interviewer will have an opportunity to contribute toward the interview (for example by being explicitly invited to do so after the lead interviewer has finished probing each topic).

A supporter may be present with the agreement of the witness to provide them with emotional support during the interview. Witness supporters cannot be other witnesses in the case. *Achieving Best Evidence* generally discourages the use of parents or carers as supporters because they can be an additional source of stress for the witness (para 2.104). Witness supporters are not appropriate adults; it has not been necessary to use appropriate adults in interviews with witnesses since para 11.15 of Code C of the Police and Criminal Evidence Act 1984 was revised on 1 April 2003.

Interpreters and intermediaries should be properly briefed and involved at an appropriate point in the interview planning process.

Intermediaries need to assess the witness before the interview to ensure that they have the skills needed to facilitate the dialogue with the witness and establish the most appropriate methods of communication during the interview. A police officer should be present during the intermediary's assessment of the witness to corroborate any unsolicited comments of relevance to the case that the witness might make. The police officer who is present during the intermediary assessment could be either the interviewer or the family liaison officer. The areas considered in an intermediary assessment vary according to the witness but they might include:

- mode of communication (verbal, visual, kinetic activity);
- extent of vocabulary (verbal/sign/symbol);
- expressive communication and language comprehension;
- auditory memory;
- attention span (including concentration);
- understanding and use of abstract and concrete words;
- likely response to open-ended and specific closed questions;
- maximum words in question;
- compliance and suggestibility;
- causality;
- time (before/after/last);
- space (in/on/over/under/in front/behind);
- ability to organize event-based information into a coherent narrative sequence.

6.6.10 **Timing, duration and pace, number of interview sessions**

The timing of the interview should take account of factors such as the witness's routine and the effects of any medication they are using (for example, if the witness has been prescribed a slow-release drug that makes them drowsy in the afternoon, the best time for the interview is likely to be the morning).

Similarly, the duration and pace of the interview must be influenced by what is known about the witness (for example, the age or medical condition of the witness might be such as to limit any interview to under an hour).

In complex cases or cases in which the witness cannot be interviewed for more than a short period of time, it may be appropriate for the interview to take place over a number of sessions. These sessions can take place over more than one day if necessary.

6.6.11 **Preparation of the witness for interview**

Witnesses should always be prepared for an interview; family liaison officers can play an important part in this process, even where they are not going to be involved in the interview. In some cases preparation can take place briefly, just before the interview; in other cases preparation might need to take place over a number of sessions several days before the interview. Interview preparation should include:

- an explanation of the role of the interviewer(s) (eg 'our role here today is to get as much detail as possible about what you saw');
- an explanation of the purpose of the interview without discussing the details of the offence being investigated (eg 'we're here today to talk about something that you told your mum that had happened to you');
- the ground rules for the interview (eg not making any assumptions about the interviewer's knowledge of what was witnessed);
- an outline of the structure of the interview without discussing the details of the offence being investigated (eg 'I'm going to start by going through a few administrative things like saying the date and time for the purposes of the record, then we'll introduce ourselves and go through a few ground rules such as reminding you to tell me if I say something you don't understand. Then I'll ask you to tell me what happened and ask you some questions about it just to make sure that I've really understood what you've said properly and so that I've got as much detail as possible');
- rapport building by means of discussing neutral topics as necessary. In cases where the witness is likely to have difficulty in understanding that the conversation rules of the interview are different to those in everyday life the discussion of neutral topics may extend to a practice interview, for example, 'to help us get used to the kind of detail that I need you to try to remember in the interview I thought that we might have a bit of a practice on something else. You've already told me that you went to see the football on Saturday. Please tell me everything that you can remember about the game.').

The interview plan should be reviewed and revised if necessary after the witness has been prepared for the interview.

6.6.12 Documentation

The plans for the interview should be written down and disclosed to the Crown Prosecution Service. An example of such a plan is set out below but it is important to remember that there is no typical plan for an interview; plans vary according to practice and circumstance.

Example interview plan

Details of witness: *John Smith (born 1.1.80)*

Summary of what is known about the witness:

30 year old white British male. No known disabilities, mental health issues or illnesses. Prefers to be called 'John'.

Type of offence: *Homicide*

How offence came to police notice: *Initially reported by 999 call from the manager of the Dog and Duck Public House, John Smith provided his details and an initial account to police after they arrived at the scene.*

Information Important to the Investigation:

Relationship between witness and suspected offender.

Objectives

1. *To confirm that John Smith was in the Dog and Duck Public House at the time of the alleged offence and the circumstances of his being there;*
2. *To establish John Smith's movements in the Dog and Duck Public House at and around the time of the alleged offence;*
3. *To find out what John Smith saw and heard in the Dog and Duck Public House at the time of the alleged offence;*
4. *To find out who else John Smith saw in the Dog and Duck Public House at the time of the alleged offence and to find out what they were doing;*
5. *To find out the nature of and background to John Smith's relationship with the suspected offender in this case, Jim Smith.*

Date, time and place of interview: *4.1.2011, 2pm, interview suite at 44 George Street*

Interviewer: *DC Fred Bloggs*

Camera Operator: *DC Jim Jones*

Interview Structure

Rapport phase: Introductions, ground rules etc. then minimal neutral topics.

Account: initiate an account of the incident in the Dog and Duck by simply asking, probe and exhaust account as per objectives 1 to 4.

Cover background material as per objective 5.

Close interview.

6.7 The Interview

Interviews that make use of the phased structure described in *Achieving Best Evidence* proceed through four phases:

1) rapport;
2) free narrative;
3) questioning;
4) closure.

It is not within the scope of this book to describe each of these phases in detail but they can be summarized briefly with reference to the diagram below.

6.7.1 Rapport

The rapport phase consists of three elements:

6.7.1.1 Preliminaries

The preliminaries to the interview include:

- covering personal introductions;
- stating the date, time and place;
- explaining the reason for the interview without mentioning the offence;
- pointing out the positions of the cameras and microphones.

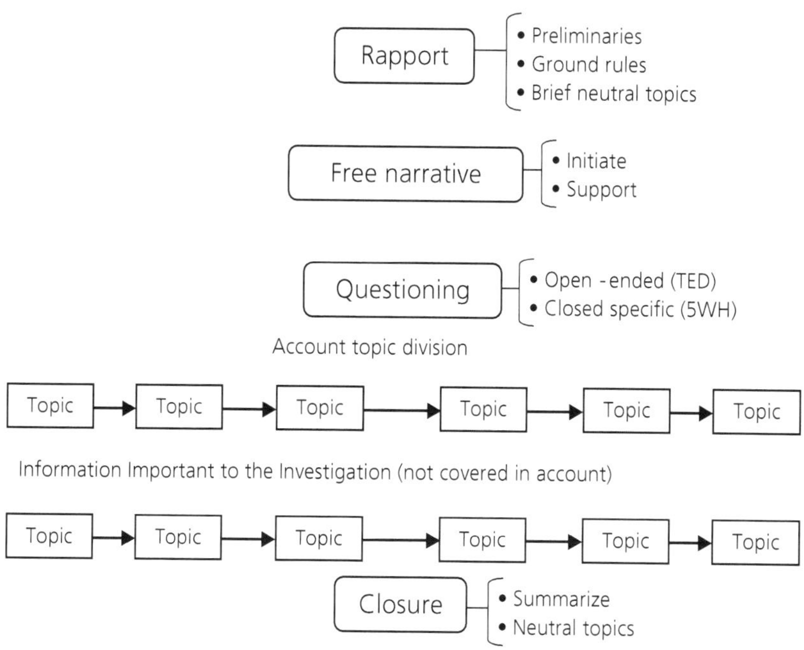

Figure 6.1 Witness interview outline

6.7.1.2 **Ground rules**

Ground rules include:

- explaining to the witness that they should try to mention everything, without editing anything out, even partial or apparently trivial detail;
- telling the witness that they should say what happened in their own way and in their own time;
- explaining to the witness that they should say if they do not understand the questions that they are asked;
- explaining to the witness that they should say if questions are asked that they do not know the answer to;
- telling the witness that they should say so if the interviewer seems to have misunderstood something that the witness told them;
- exploring the witness's understanding of truth and lies if they are under 17 (under 18 when s 98 of the Coroners and Justice Act 2009 is implemented) or have a learning disability;

6.7.1.3 **Neutral topics**

A discussion focusing on neutral topics such as the witness's hobbies and pastimes is intended to serve two purposes:

1) to create a relaxed atmosphere, as far as possible, given the circumstances;
2) to give the witness the opportunity to practice the unusual conversational rules that applies to an investigative interview, where necessary.

Any discussion of neutral topics should be brief. Where a lengthier discussion is necessary to build rapport between the witness and the interviewer (as may be the case with some young children, or witnesses with learning disabilities or trauma) it should take place when the witness is prepared for the interview, over more than one session if necessary.

6.7.2 **Free narrative**

The free-narrative phase consists of two elements:

1) initiation;
2) supporting.

In many instances free narrative is initiated by means of an open-ended prompt such as 'tell me what happened last night?' It is then sustained by means of active listening techniques and open-ended prompts such as echo questions.

6.7.3 **Questioning**

The questioning phase consists of:

1) dividing the witness's account into relevant manageable topics;
2) systematically probing each topic that was not fully covered during the free-narrative phase by inviting the witness to recapitulate on it in more depth before the interviewer moves on to probe it with open-ended then specific-closed questions;
3) systematically probing topics of information important to the investigation that have not already been covered in the witness's account.

Whether any given question that is used is open-ended or specific-closed depends largely on context but, in general terms, open-ended questions are typically (though not exclusively) those beginning with 'tell me …', 'explain to me …', or 'describe to me …' (sometimes referred to as TED questions) whereas specific-closed questions often (though not always) begin with 'who', 'what', 'where', 'when', 'why', or 'how' (sometimes referred to a 5WH questions).

Forced-choice questions such as 'was it hot or was it cold?' should generally be avoided because the choices given may not include the correct alternative. In circumstances where forced-choice questions are unavoidable (eg where a witness's disabilities or injuries are so severe as to limit a witness's communication skills to only being able to respond 'yes' or 'no' to a question) a third alternative such as 'don't know' or 'neither of those' should ideally be included.

Leading questions should also be avoided. A leading question is one that is either phrased in such a way as to indicate the kind of answer that the questioner wants (eg 'I bet that hurt, didn't it?'). Alternatively, a question might be regarded as leading if it introduces something into the interview that has not already been mentioned by the witness, particularly where such information might be disputed later on in court. An example of this second kind of leading question might be 'how did you get that bruise' when the question is asked before a competent medical practitioner has declared that it is a bruise and not some other kind of mark.

The final type of question to be avoided is the multiple question. When such questions are asked it can be difficult to know what part of the question the witness's response refers to. For example:

> Question: 'did he only hit you twice or did he hit you more than that?'
> Answer: 'Yes'

In these circumstances the interviewer invariably has to ask another question to clarify the ambiguity in the response.

6.7.4 Closure

The closure phase consists of:

- brief communication between interviewers and between the interviewers and interview monitor to ensure that no more questions need to be asked;
- summarizing what the witness has said;
- answering any questions from the witness;
- asking the witness to contact the investigation team if they remember anything else about the incident;
- returning to neutral topics if necessary;
- reporting the end-time of the interview for the purposes of the video/audio recording.

6.8 Chapter Summary

This chapter has considered the assessment and interviewing of witnesses in the family. The knowledge that family liaison officers are likely to have about the offence is likely to mean that they will rarely be used as interviewers. Their knowledge and experience of the witness and the family dynamics are such, however, that interviewers who do not actively solicit a contribution from the family liaison officer when they plan the interview are certainly 'missing a trick'.

Regardless of whether the family liaison officer interviews a witness in the family, it is important that they have a sound grasp of the interview process so that they can help to prepare the witness for the interview and address any concerns that they might have either before or after it has taken place.

References

Association of Chief Police Officers, *Practical Guide to Investigative Interviewing* (Wyboston, Centrex, 2004)

Association of Chief Police Officers and Home Office, *Vulnerable Witnesses: A Police Service Guide* (London, Home Office, 2001)

Office for Criminal Justice Reform, *Code of Practice for Victims of Crime* (London, Office for Criminal Justice Reform, 2005)

Office for Criminal Justice Reform, *Achieving Best Evidence in Criminal Proceedings: Guidance on Interviewing Victims and Witnesses, and Using Special Measures* (London, Office for Criminal Justice Reform, 2007)

Office for Criminal Justice Reform, *Witness Charter* (London, Office for Criminal Justice Reform, 2007)

NOTES

NOTES

7

Coroners' Processes

7.1 Introduction

Family liaison officers should at the earliest opportunity provide to the family an explanation of coroners' processes. In homicide cases in England and Wales this can be facilitated by helping the family to go through the following sections of *Information for the Bereaved* (Office for Criminal Justice Reform, 2009):

- identifying and viewing the deceased person;
- the inquest;
- understanding the role of the coroner and the coroner's officers;
- understanding the purpose of a post-mortem examination;
- the funeral.

Other sections of *Information for the Bereaved*, such as giving consent for donating tissues and organs and obtaining personal possessions of the deceased person, may be referred to as appropriate.

In cases involving a death on the road reference should be made to *Information and Advice for Bereaved Families and Friends following Death on the Road in England and Wales* (Brake, 2009). The following sections of this document are of particular relevance to coroners' processes:

- what happens to a loved one's body;
- burials or cremations;
- inquests.

The purpose of this chapter is briefly to outline these processes to assist family liaison officers to fulfil this aspect of their role.

7.2 Explaining Coroners' Processes

Family liaison officers are responsible for explaining the procedures associated with:

- viewing the body;
- identifying the body;
- the inquest;
- the release of the body.

KEY POINT – FAMILY LIAISON OFFICER'S RESPONSIBILITIES

Family liaison officers are responsible for explaining the following procedures:

- viewing the body;
- identifying the body;
- the inquest;
- the release of the body.

While it is reasonable to provide the family with a general overview of these procedures, advice from coroners' officers about the particular procedures that are applicable to the case under investigation should always be sought before discussing them in depth with the family so as to avoid raising unrealistic expectations.

7.3 Viewing the Body

Viewing the body and the identification procedure are separate processes that should not be confused with one another. The nature of the identification procedure in any given case is determined by the coroner; it will not always be a matter of visual identification. The family may, however, want to view the body regardless of whether identification is to take place on a visual basis.
Prior to arranging a viewing the family liaison officer should:

- consult the SIO or the SIM to ensure that forensic issues are unlikely to be compromised as a result of the viewing;
- view the deceased independently of the family to ascertain the condition of the body, including any injuries. Where it is thought to be appropriate, consideration could be given to showing the family a photograph of the deceased to prepare them for the viewing but family liaison officers should not express an opinion on whether a viewing is appropriate or not; some families may feel that a viewing could have a long-term benefit on the grieving process, even though they are likely to find it a difficult experience at the time;
- visit the mortuary and establish which parts of the premises the family will have access to;
- where injuries to the body have occurred as a result of the post-mortem, discuss the post-mortem procedure with the coroner's officer and then talk to the family about the need for this procedure before the viewing;
- where the family may want to touch the deceased or perform cultural rituals in respect of the body while at the mortuary, seek the advice of the coroner's officer;
- arrange the viewing with the coroner's officer, and ask him or her to make sure that the body is in as presentable condition as is possible.

Viewing the body is clearly going to be a difficult time for the family and police managers should be aware of the possibility that family liaison officers may experience some vicarious trauma as a result of the time that they spend with the family during the viewing.

7.4 Identification of the Body

Coroners have a statutory responsibility for identification; they decide which methods are to be used to identify the deceased. Given that the nature of identification varies from case to case, family liaison officers should only discuss the process with the family after they have spoken to the coroner's officer about it.

While visual identification of the deceased is the most common method used, it is not likely to be possible where injuries are extensive or where significant decomposition has occurred. In these circumstances the options open to the coroner include the use of:

- dental charting;
- DNA;
- fingerprints.

In some circumstances the coroner may also consider other invasive or even mutilative techniques, such as the removal of body parts.

Whatever the method of identification, the family liaison officer will need to provide a clear and candid explanation of the rationale for it to the family.

7.5 The Inquest

The role of the coroner and the purpose of an inquest is to determine the identity of the deceased, when and where death occurred, and the cause of death and how, and in what circumstances, it occurred. It is not the role of the inquest to decide who is to blame for the death; it is not a trial, but a limited enquiry into the facts surrounding the death.

The initial hearing is usually adjourned after the deceased has been formally identified and the brief circumstances of the death have been outlined. The family need not attend this hearing but should be given the option of doing so. The family liaison officer should discuss the initial hearing with the family after having consulted the coroner's officer.

After someone has been charged with causing the death the inquest remains adjourned until the outcome of the criminal trial is known. The inquest is not usually resumed when there is a conviction because the crown court trial effectively replaces the inquest. The inquest will resume if the person who has been charged is not convicted; in these circumstances the coroner's officer prepares a file of evidence that relies on the material obtained during the police investigation.

7.6 The Release of the Body

The coroner is responsible for releasing the body and will usually only do so to the next of kin. Prior to releasing the body the coroner will need to be satisfied that the post-mortem examination is complete and that any potential further post-mortems have either taken place or are unlikely to be necessary.

KEY POINT – ADVICE FROM THE CORONER'S OFFICER

Family liaison officers should obtain advice from the coroner's officer about the application of coronial processes to any given case to reduce the possibility of them inadvertently giving rise to unrealistic expectations on the part of the family about matters such as the timing of the release of the body.

7.7 Chapter Summary

It is the family liaison officer's role to explain the coronial processes associated with the viewing of the body, identifying the body, the inquest and the release of the body. This chapter has briefly outlined these processes with a view to assisting family liaison officers with this aspect of their role.

NOTES

NOTES

8

Mass Fatalities and Ante Mortem Collection

8.1 Introduction

In the UK the responsibility for collecting ante mortem data following a disaster rests with the police service. The UK police are members of the Interpol Steering Group on Disaster Victim Identification (DVI). The steering group consists of a number of police forces in Europe and throughout the world who collaborate on techniques that will enhance the ability of their countries to make a speedy identification of its citizens following a major disaster where mass fatalities are incurred. The UK model of police family liaison is a fairly unique concept in mass fatalities; many of the other Interpol states use other agents to capture data.

The ante mortem data to be collected includes the data from the people who know the most about the missing person, as well as the forensic data and material that could provide a valuable link that leads to an identification. The purpose of this chapter is to outline how this process works and to show how the implementation of a system in the UK that utilizes family liaison has helped develop a quicker, more reliable way of obtaining ante mortem data that assists the work that is done by body recovery teams, mortuary documentation teams, casualty bureau staff, major incident rooms and, ultimately, an identification commission.

8.2 Community Confidence and Police Family Liaison

The relationship between the police and the community is rarely more important than in times of crisis. There is inevitably high interest from all media, especially the 24-hour news channels. This often creates an environment in which interviews with witnesses, 'experts', families and people who have previously been affected by major disasters are broadcast around the clock and there is a great deal of speculation by commentators on matters such as the cause of the event that led to the crisis, the number of casualties etc. At times like this families and communities look to the lead agencies for quality, timely information, leadership, support and well-practised strategies, which will facilitate their recovery from the psychological impact of the disaster. It is important that the quality of the family liaison officers' communication is of such a high standard that the families' primary source of information is the police rather than the speculative reporting that is sometimes published in newspapers and broadcast on the news channels.

Experience in the UK has shown that failure to respond appropriately in the immediate aftermath of a traumatic event can leave scars on families and communities that may never heal. There is a need for all agencies to respond at the highest possible level of efficiency and compassion. The racist murder of Stephen Lawrence, a young black man, in London in 1993 brought about an organizational crisis within the police service. The resultant public inquiry exposed failings in how the police dealt with families in the aftermath of fatal incidents. Running in parallel to this process was the build up to another public inquiry; this one involved a public transport disaster in which 51 young people had lost their lives on the pleasure cruiser 'The Marchioness' on the River Thames in London on 20 August 1989. After years of campaigning by many of the families whose loved ones had died in this incident a public inquiry was held to look at the issues surrounding the incident itself as well as how post and ante mortem procedures take place in the UK. The way that the lead authorities communicate with families in these circumstances and the level of honest information that they provided was also examined. It soon became apparent that the families felt badly let down by the police liaison, among other things, and, even though the police were able to show that they had made great efforts to improve since these terrible events, the public inquiry exposed failings and suggested that they still had a long way to go.

A great deal of development has now taken place in the use of police family liaison in mass disaster and it has proved effective in many major incidents including the attacks on the World Trade Center, the Bali terrorist attacks, the Asian tsunami, the London bombings, and other domestic and international disasters.

8.3 Disaster and Police Family Liaison

On 5 October 1999 a train crash occurred just outside Ladbroke Grove railway station in central London. While the investigation and recovery operation eventually established that 31 people had died and many more had been injured, the extent of the devastation of the front carriages of the train influenced initial suggestions made in highly speculative early media reports that the death toll could be as high as 500. The resulting unprecedented media coverage was an issue for family liaison during the recovery operation; it was very difficult to keep families apprised of genuine updates when rumours and speculation were being beamed directly into their homes via 24-hour news stations.

At this time there were no written protocols for the deployment of family liaison officers in mass fatality incidents because it was not clear whether this was a police investigation or a recovery following a tragic accident. Police body recovery experts were, however, being used and the police Casualty Bureau had been opened, with an emergency number being released to worried relatives and friends so that they could call if they were concerned about someone that they had been unable to contact.

When the Ladbroke Grove train crash took place the police service was still recovering from the Stephen Lawrence inquiry criticisms while the publication of 'The Marchioness' public inquiry, with further criticisms about how the police service dealt with families following death in tragic circumstances, was imminent. These factors influenced the decision to deploy police family liaison officers for the first time to a disaster in the UK.

In the first 48 hours after the crash 111 police family liaison officers were deployed to families and survivors. Police family liaison officers are not intended to be deployed solely to perform a welfare function; they should only ever be used if the deployment serves an investigative function. Initially, their function in the investigation that followed the Ladbroke Grove rail crash was to liaise with the families who had reported people missing with a view to confirming whether their loved ones had actually been on the train. Having confirmed that the missing person had been on the train, the family liaison officers investigated the possibility that they had been injured and were in hospital or were otherwise unable to make contact with their family. After establishing that the missing person was not in hospital or otherwise unable to contact their family, family liaison officers collected the kind of material that could, in the worst circumstances, aid the identification of a deceased person who had been recovered from the scene of the crash. Casualty Bureau had managed to prioritize the list of the missing by putting several hundred reports into a grading system. The top grade was that the missing person:

1) was thought to have been definitely on the train, with some supporting evidence to corroborate that fact, eg someone had watched them actually board the train;
2) did not feature on any of the lists of the injured people who were being treated at any of the six hospitals being used; and
3) had not been heard from since the crash despite persistent attempts by family and friends to trace them through phone calls to personal mobiles, places of business where they might be heading etc.

The next grade down was that there was supporting evidence to say that they were very likely to have been on the train. Not everyone who got on the train was seen by someone who knew them. Many people who ended up in the highest category started off in the lower 'possibly involved' category until enquiries to trace them had been made without success and time had elapsed without them contacting anybody.

Family liaison officers were deployed to all families falling within the top category and the next category down from it. Officers were briefed and equipped with the appropriate documentation required to obtain full descriptive details of the families' missing loved ones.

In a capital city as cosmopolitan as London it is highly likely that foreign nationals will also be caught up in an incident of this scale. It was, therefore, important that the response to this incident conformed to international policing protocols for the identification and repatriation of deceased citizens. Such protocols are intended to ensure that there is a thorough system in place that should avoid any mistakes in identification. The UK's relationship with the Interpol Steering Group on Disaster Victim Identification (DVI) is important because it facilitates communication between the key individuals responsible for DVI in the foreign countries involved and this maximizes the ability of the

UK police to gather and share ante mortem information around the world quickly and effectively.

Complexities in identification often follow a mass fatality incident due to the high incidence of body fragmentation. It is highly unlikely in the aftermath of a mass fatality incident in the UK that a coroner (or, in Scotland, a Procurator Fiscal) will allow any identification to be made visually. This does not prevent the families seeing their loved ones. Viewings are usually facilitated at a viewing area near the mortuary as soon after the identification has been made as practicable. Separating the identification process from a viewing in this way is intended to ensure that any identification is made via a robust process that does not result in errors and that mistaken identification never occurs. The primary sources of identification need to be robustly checked and corroborated as a result. Dental records, DNA, fingerprints or some unique medical factors are the best and most acceptable means of identification. This, however, involves asking families many sensitive questions on a range of personal issues; a great understanding of both the families' tragedy and the work of the responding agencies is crucial in these circumstances. It is, therefore, essential that the expertise of the family liaison officer is not only in the sensitive gathering of crucial, accurate data and forensic exhibits in extraordinary circumstances but in the way that they are able to explain to the family the inner workings of identification procedures, the investigation into the incident and the coronial and criminal justice systems.

8.4 Lessons from Ladbroke Grove

A debrief of the family liaison officers was held a month after the Ladbroke Grove rail disaster and a range of positive comments were made and concerns raised by the practitioners. These fell into the following categories:

- training;
- deployment;
- logistics;
- welfare;
- future planning.

8.4.1 Training

Some of the officers felt that the training that had previously been provided was not effective in preparing them for an incident of this nature because no consideration had been given in it to the possibility of their engagement in a mass fatality investigation. This was a fair point. The training of Metropolitan Police family liaison officers had been designed following the Stephen Lawrence inquiry. While there was some generic material in it about dealing with a viewing of the deceased and working with bereaved people, there was nothing about the differences between a homicide or road death investigation and one where a high number of casualties are involved. There were some significant differences between these types of investigations. Such differences were particularly significant in terms of the paper flow systems, and the internal police disciplines and external partners that they worked with. Additional training was also necessary in respect of obtaining consent from families for the release of medical information and new forms had to be designed for this purpose. When someone dies in circumstances where their body is not identifiable by traditional means it can often be the smallest detail that expedites identification. Obtaining someone's medical history may be extremely important. The kind of details that might be included are blood grouping, medical conditions that the deceased person may have suffered from, operations that left a mark or scar and possibly some record of any samples of blood or fluid that may have been retained by the relevant medical authorities.

Many of the family liaison officers also felt that more training on how to exit from the family in mass fatality investigations was required. In a homicide investigation there is usually a 'road map' with significant points along the way. When someone is charged and a trial is being prepared contact with the family should change from a full investigative process to maintaining the flow of information to the family to keep them informed about the progress of the case. The police should be looking at partner agencies to have a far greater role in

KEY POINT – FAMILY LIAISON TRAINING FOR MASS FATALITIES

Training family liaison officers to perform the role in connection with homicide and road death investigations will not prepare them for mass fatality situations. The training of family liaison officers should, therefore, include some material on the differences between investigations involving one or a few fatalities and an investigation involving mass fatalities including:

- differences between the paper flow systems of homicide/road death investigations and those of investigations into mass fatalities;
- differences between the internal police disciplines involved in an investigation into mass fatalities and those involved in homicide/road death investigations;
- differences between the external partners in an investigation into mass fatalities and those in homicide/road death investigations;
- differences between the approach taken by the criminal justice system towards mass fatalities and the way it approaches homicide/road death;
- issues to do with obtaining consent from families for the release of medical information in mass fatality investigations;
- the kind of details that might facilitate identification when the body is not immediately identifiable;
- exit strategies for mass fatality investigations.

supporting relatives by this time. Mass fatality incidents have fewer 'signposts' and it is often a far slower process after an inquest is opened; this proved to be difficult for family liaison officers in the aftermath of Ladbroke Grove. As is explained later in this chapter, the importance of forging better relationships with partner agencies following a mass fatality incident was firmly established as a result of the experience of family liaison officers following the Ladbroke Grove rail crash.

New training was also needed to cover the fact that the journey through the criminal justice system for a family is different in mass fatalities than it is in cases of homicide or road death.

8.4.2 **Deployment**

There were concerns about the efficiency of the call-out system for family liaison officers in an emergency and the negotiation that was required with line managers for the release to the investigation team dealing with a major incident of locally employed staff. This indicated that training had to be extended beyond the family liaison officer to those who manage, supervise and support them. As a consequence the roles of family liaison co-ordinator and family liaison advisor were developed. These roles are fundamental to success in a major disaster. Some problems still occur with family liaison officers being released from core roles to take on their role in a major incident. The only way that these can be resolved is by means of a family liaison structure in the organization that supports police delivery of this service. It has to be driven top down as well as bottom up. It is no coincidence that the most effective forces in delivering family liaison in the UK happen to be the ones with the most effective family liaison coordinators.

While there was criticism of the team structure at the beginning, there was praise for the subsequent development that involved the setting up of small teams of family liaison officers. Each of these small teams was led by a team leader with their own clearly understood responsibilities.

8.4.3 **Logistics**

The logistical issues that arose from Ladbroke Grove related to communication and transport.

8.4.3.1 **Communication**

The initial communication problems dramatically improved when the family liaison officers were supplied with mobile telephones and pagers. Overall, however, communication between the family liaison officers and the other disciplines who responded to the incident was poor; this was partly because other investigators were unfamiliar with family liaison as it was a new aspect of the police response to a major disaster incident.

It should also be remembered that communication is going to be difficult in an emergency. A plan needs to be implemented that overcomes these problems. Mobile networks get very busy and the result can be that the systems crash. Setting up a briefing room where staff can meet and be given information is essential. The location of the incident must be taken into account when considering any problems that might occur in respect of travel. These issues should be planned for in advance, something that did not happen at Ladbroke Grove because the involvement of family liaison in mass disaster was new at the time.

8.4.3.2 **Transport**

The family liaison officers also had transportation problems at the beginning. While many of the responders will by necessity be located at or near the disaster itself, this was not so for the family liaison officers whose role it was to trace relatives and friends wherever they were and gather the ante mortem data urgently.

KEY POINT – FAMILY LIAISON LOGISTICS IN MASS FATALITY INVESTIGATIONS

It is essential that the following issues are resolved when family liaison officers are deployed in mass fatality investigations:

- communication:
  - issuing mobile telephones to family liaison officers;
  - an understanding by others involved in the investigation of the role of the family liaison officer;
- transport:
  - alternative arrangements may need to be made for family liaison officers to travel to and from families when transport systems are affected by a mass fatality incident.

8.4.4 **Welfare**

It was recognized that support systems needed to be built for major incidents over and above those designed for normal business. Many family liaison officers had to spend periods of time away from home and that brought problems as to how to manage the competing demands of home and work. Extra provisions have to be made to keep staff safe and healthy and to allow business to run smoothly. It was suggested that between major incidents there should be regular 'team meetings' where good practice could be exchanged and working relationships could be developed in 'peace time'.

8.4.5 Future planning

Family liaison officers requested that a service policy be developed with protocols that were understood by all. This was a fundamental acceptance that family liaison was there to stay in mass fatalities and that there was a need to plan and prepare for the next time. There was an acknowledgment that this could not be done in isolation but had to be developed alongside the other disciplines who respond to mass fatalities. In family liaison this would mean engaging with external agencies as well as police partners.

8.5 The Development of the Family Liaison Officer Role in Mass Fatality Investigations

As the newest police discipline in mass fatalities, the 'ante mortem' collection team became exposed to many disasters over the next few years.

8.5.1 New York 2001

The events of 11 September 2001 drew a family liaison response from the UK and several teams of family liaison officers were sent to New York in the months following the attack on the World Trade Center. Their role was to assist the New York authorities on behalf of the UK government to identify and repatriate any UK citizens killed in the attack. This was achieved through the collection of ante mortem data from the affected UK families along with any medical information and transporting it according to international protocols to those entrusted with the identification of the dead, namely the City of New York Office of the Chief Medical Examiner. It was another significant 'first' for police family liaison. The discipline was now considered to be core business and, as such, had become a key deployment in what was a homicide, terrorist attack, major disaster and mass fatality incident. It was also abroad and the UK police could only get involved in the US if they were invited to do so by the American authorities, and they had to work to very strict guidelines while they were there.

There were difficulties in setting up a UK police mission in the US. As with Ladbroke Grove, communication was fundamental to success. One of the logistical problems was the fact that there was a five-hour time difference between offices in the UK and the police mission in the US. This was a problem that had to be resolved because having only a finite pool of staff meant that working lengthy hours was neither desirable nor feasible. The problem was resolved by setting up a small overlapping shift system. In addition to this, setting up a communication system so that one point of contact in London only liaised with one point of contact in New York made a massive difference to delivering a consistent standard of service and avoiding unnecessary duplication. All the enquiries from London were channelled through one point and received at the single point of contact in Manhattan and vice versa.

Working in another country, another continent, was not easy for staff. Many had work commitments that could not be sustained through a prolonged absence from local business. Many had family commitments that would possibly impact on their own welfare. The key to successfully managing this issue was the same as it had been in Ladbroke Grove; effective supervision and support as well as welfare provision during and after the event. A team of bereavement volunteers from a charity called CRUSE was sent out to assist with the UK police mission. This allowed the family liaison officers to leave the families with trained helpers after the investigative work had been completed. The Metropolitan Police Service also sent out a team from their Occupational Health Department to New York. This team gave the officers involved in the delivery of family liaison an opportunity to discuss their experiences on a daily basis. This was something that proved invaluable and should be a consideration if any such deployments are ever undertaken in the future.

8.5.2 **Bali 2002**

A similar protocol was applied to the terrorist attacks in Bali, Indonesia in October 2002. In this incident the UK government supported an investigation that was led by Indonesian and Australian law enforcement officials by sending a UK family liaison/ante mortem collection team. While the team working in Indonesia was an important part of the plan, it was only part of an overall strategy that was intended to locate potential ante mortem information wherever it could be found. In the response to New York and Bali, family liaison teams worked in the UK simultaneously with those deployed overseas so that any data or forensic material could be gathered and forwarded without delay should it become available.

One of the aspects of this deployment that warranted special consideration was 'risk assessment'. In New York the risk to British police staff was minimized after assurances were obtained from the American authorities. Obtaining such assurances was not as easy in Indonesia and there were times where the British team felt that they may be potential targets for further terrorist attacks. This was something that should ideally have been managed before deployment as opposed to afterwards when family liaison officers were already locally engaged.

The climate was another issue that was a potential hazard. The welfare of the family liaison officers included additional efforts to keep the team healthy in an extremely hot working environment. In addition to this, members of the family liaison team needed to be inoculated before deployment. The fact that it takes a few days for the inoculations to take effect sometimes meant that the available pool of staff shrunk drastically to only those experienced family liaison officers who had already been inoculated.

8.5.3 **The Asian tsunami 2004**

The events of 26 December 2004 were unprecedented across the world and unique again to the domestic police service in the UK. The UK DVI response was to send teams of appropriately trained officers to Thailand to assist in a truly international and multi-disciplinary response. It would be fair to say that it was some time before an effective family liaison/ante mortem plan kicked in properly. Much of the early response was taken up with call-handling as UK citizens who were worried about their friends and relatives reported their concerns to the police Casualty Bureau.

It took some time for the call-handling to become manageable due to the extremely high volume. Only then was a true picture able to emerge as to where the friends and relatives of those missing were. It became clear that they were not concentrated in one area. As a result, all UK police forces needed to come together to deal with the collection of ante mortem data. From a police family liaison point of view it was clear that a regional plan was required. The family liaison plan was to separate into regions that were akin to the working regions applied by the Association of Chief Police Officers. This was fairly easy to administer because these regions had working relationships anyway and the family liaison coordinators and advisors were known to each other.

Each region then took on a number of missing persons to investigate. The region became responsible for the full investigation into each missing person to include the collection of statements, ante mortem data, forensic exhibits etc. The collection would be done to the standards required in Thailand where the UK had representation within the International Information Management Centre that was based in Phuket. Regional information was then quality assured locally before being transported and received in London. From there it was transferred into Thailand.

The main lesson from the family liaison response to the tsunami was that due to the sheer volume of activity many police family liaison officers were used who had not been previously trained to respond to mass fatalities. It had never been anticipated that the domestic police would have to respond on such a scale and most forces found that they did not have the resilience in DVI-trained family liaison officers to cope with a disaster on this scale. This is something that has now been addressed and DVI training for all family liaison officers has been available as a national package to all forces in the UK since 2008. Prior to the development of the national package training was available but it was not to a consistent national standard. This may have contributed to a variation in practice, which in turn led to quality control issues.

8.5.4 **London 2005**

In many ways the London bombs showed how many lessons the emerging discipline of family liaison had learnt and an effective response commenced immediately. Included in this response was a new development in the UK, the establishment of a family assistance centre (FAC) or, as it was known in London on 7 July 2005, a humanitarian assistance centre.

The multi-agency centre was modelled on the family assistance centre that had been opened in Manhattan in the days and months following the attacks on the World Trade Center. The overall intention was to provide a 'one-stop shop' for people affected by the attacks. It provided an added dimension to the family liaison response in as much as family liaison officers were able to trace relatives and friends who were proving difficult to contact at their homes. As often happens in a disaster, relatives made their way to the place where the incident occurred to try to find out more about what had happened. This is totally understandable and the authorities should take care to provide information, shelter and assistance to people when this occurs. Unfortunately one consequence of the families need to go to the area can be difficulties for the family liaison officers in contacting them with a view to gathering ante mortem data. Having the capability to interview and capture data *wherever the family are* becomes a major step forward in making identifications quicker without losing quality of data.

8.6 The Ante Mortem Information that Family Liaison Officers Need to Collect

8.6.1 Dental

In order to comply with international protocols it is likely that the family liaison officers will be asked to complete the ante mortem section of the Interpol DVI forms. The other half of these forms will be completed at the mortuary and the aim will be to find enough data to allow a forensic match to be made between the ante mortem and post-mortem forms.

Families should be asked for their permission to access dental records because they are extremely important when trying to make an accurate identification. When released by dentists, original records can be examined by odontologists and compared against the deceased person's mortuary photographs and dental charts. This can take some time to organize so the family liaison officers need to get written permission as soon as possible from the family along with the details of all the dental practitioners used by the deceased.

Photographs are also important to the identification process, particularly if they show a good clear recent picture of the missing person smiling and showing their teeth. A good investigation should be able to gain information from families about where such pictures may be found. This could be from friends they went on holiday with, partners, ex partners, work colleagues or ex work colleagues etc. Family liaison officers need a comprehensive understanding of what could be useful and where to find it.

Once gathered, all material needs to be recorded and preserved appropriately by the family liaison officer according to investigative standards and the forensic strategy as set by the senior identification manager (SIM) or DVI commander.

8.6.2 **DNA**

While extremely important, DNA is not always going to be the best method of identification. It needs to be recovered and stored while decisions are made about the forensic strategy for the investigation. A forensic adviser could make a very useful contribution to a family liaison team in the aftermath of a disaster. The family liaison officers may have to identify potential opportunities for recovering DNA and that is an area where advice from a forensic adviser could be extremely useful. If DNA is to be used to establish identity, the family liaison officer will have to prepare a comprehensive lineage chart or 'family tree' in order that the best advice is taken about from whom the family liaison officer should obtain a DNA swab. This will minimize duplication of work as well as avoiding the needless swabbing of individuals who are unlikely to yield a positive result.

At all times the family liaison officer needs to keep the family aware of the processes involved and to avoid raising their expectations in respect of timescales. This is an agonizing time for the families and information from the police is very important to them. The family liaison officer must remember that they are competing with speculative 24-hour media coverage. It is, therefore, especially important to develop and to adhere to a plan for disclosing accurate information to the family at this difficult time.

Places where DNA may be gathered include:

- clothing (unwashed preferably);
- toothbrush;
- cups or mugs;
- letters or envelopes that the missing person has sealed;
- bedding;
- telephone, especially one used exclusively by the missing person;
- skin cells trapped inside the links of a watch.

These may be gathered from the home, place of work, lockers at the gym, inside a motor vehicle, from a pre existing database etc. Finding out whether someone has ever given blood is also likely to be important. This list is not exhaustive by any means and finding out about the missing person will yield further clues as to where forensic evidence may be found.

In order that opportunities are not missed, a thorough investigation of the lifestyle and routine of the missing person is required because it can make the contribution from the family liaison officer, as supported by the family liaison coordinator/advisor and forensic expert, absolutely central to the process of identification.

8.6.3 **Fingerprints**

As with DNA capture, success in obtaining fingerprints can depend on knowing as much as possible about the lifestyle and routine of the missing person. A forensic advisor can assist family liaison officers in identifying where good quality fingerprints are most likely to be found by explaining the type of surfaces that may yield a positive result. On any visit to the family home the family liaison officer may even have to ask families to hand over valuable and precious items for forensic examination. Where such a request is made it is important that an explanation is given to the family about what forensic examination could do to the item and whether it can be returned to them later on in the same state as it was given; forensic advice should be obtained in this regard whenever necessary. A balance has to be struck between identification and the preservation of precious family items. That is why a dialogue about forensic processes must take place between police and the family. Family liaison officers should record the family's wishes in their log book and submit that log book for supervision on a regular basis.

Family liaison officers can obtain advice on the return of property and many other important issues from the website of the registered charity Disaster Action (<www.disasteraction.org.uk>). This charity is run by survivors and bereaved people from previous disasters and provides invaluable advice to responders. It primarily serves as a support point for people affected by the disaster and is a superb resource to which to refer relatives and friends in the aftermath of a mass fatality incident in the UK or abroad. The website also serves as a very useful resource to police practitioners in the aftermath of a major disaster.

It may be necessary for the family liaison officer to find a way of preserving fingerprints until a forensic expert has examined them. Families may feel the need to tidy or dust an area in the hope that their loved one will return home safely. It is important to ask the family and friends to identify places that no one other than the missing person has touched. In the event that a number of people have touched the area, elimination fingerprints will need to be taken from all. The forensic strategy for the incident needs to address the requirement to have forensic examiners available throughout the UK at very short notice in order that any potential forensic opportunities are captured without delay.

8.6.4 **Distinctive medical characteristics**

Another area for family liaison officers to consider is whether the missing person had any distinctive medical characteristics. These can include unusual scars, but even these can be inconclusive since other people may have had similar medical interventions. Identification can obviously be greatly assisted if it is known that the missing person has had a medical procedure that has left a unique trace, for example an artificial limb or a body part that bears a serial number recorded by the hospital or the medical practitioner that fitted it.

Heart pacemakers should also have a unique identifier. The more in depth the family liaison officer can be when interviewing friends and relatives the better the opportunity of an early and accurate identification.

It is very unlikely that hospitals or doctors surgeries will release material without signed approval from a next of kin, so release forms are vital to the process. For example, x-rays recovered from a hospital can sometimes show a unique or unusual condition, for example where someone has previously broken a limb that has not repaired properly.

8.6.5 Other supporting information

Information on clothing and jewellery must be recorded on the ante mortem DVI forms. This could provide valuable though not conclusive information that could assist identification. It would be wrong to identify someone simply as a result of an item in their possession. They could easily have found it before the incident. There is very little in the way of unique clothing, although it can help to find out as much information about what someone was wearing as possible. Where it was purchased as well as size, stains, rips, replacement buttons etc. can all make a useful contribution to identification. The same can be said of jewellery with particular attention to inscriptions bearing names and dates if there are any. Photographs of the clothing and/or jewellery being worn should be asked for and, failing that, pictures of the same item in a catalogue can be of assistance.

Full descriptions of tattoos need to be recorded, ideally with a good clear photograph showing them. The exact location of the tattoo needs to be charted on the ante mortem form along with the tattooist's details and the approximate date and place etc. where the tattoo was obtained. Tattooists often have a catalogue of their work and may even have photographs.

KEY POINT – ANTE MORTEM INFORMATION NEEDED IN A MASS FATALITY INVESTIGATION

Family liaison officers need to consider the following ante mortem information during a mass fatality investigation:

- dental records;
- DNA material;
- fingerprints;
- distinctive medical characteristics;
- other supporting information (including tattoos, clothing and jewellery).

8.7 Chapter Summary

Ultimately the DVI process will guide family liaison officers into the important areas where investigation is important. Their investigative experience and training in the area of mass fatalities as well as their professionalism when dealing with traumatized bereaved relatives will add a dimension to identification and recovery. This dimension was not present in the UK before the Ladbroke Grove rail disaster. The coming together of disciplines in this area since 1999 has been driven by good leadership in a period that served up unprecedented challenges. We can, however, always do better and after all:

> At the very worst time of their lives
> The very least we can do
> Is our very best

Duncan McGarry, *Humanitarian Assistance in Emergencies: Guidance on Establishing Humanitarian Assistance Centres* (Cabinet Office/ACPO, 2006)

NOTES

NOTES

NOTES

9

Critical Incidents

9.1 Introduction

There are a number of areas outside homicide, road death and mass fatality where police family liaison has made a positive contribution to the investigative strategy.

Critical incidents have always been included in any guidance for family liaison as being an area where a family liaison strategy could benefit the police response.

The definition of 'critical incident' comes from guidance that has been developed by the Metropolitan Police Service, set out in *Managing and Preventing Critical Incidents Manual VII* (MPS, 2006) and subsequently adopted nationally in England and Wales by the Association of Chief Police Officers (see *Practice Advice on Critical Incident Management* (ACPO, 2007)).

KEY POINT—DEFINITION OF A CRITICAL INCIDENT

Any incident where the effectiveness of the police response is likely to have a significant impact on the confidence of:

- the victim;
- their family; *and/or*
- the community.

As can be seen from this definition, there is an emphasis on maintaining public confidence in policing. The measure that is used within this guidance is 'the effectiveness' of the police response, specifically with victims, families and communities. This modern theme in policing encourages us to view the nature of 'effective' policing and 'effective' investigation as something that can be considered in terms of the confidence that it instils in the clients of the police service, the public. While the family are very much the clients of family liaison it would be foolish to ignore the effects on it of good or bad policing in the wider community.

The identification by the police of a potential critical incident at the earliest possible stage is likely to maximize the options that are available to deal with it. While most of the incidents that are routinely dealt with by the police service on a daily basis are unlikely to ever result in a loss of public confidence and become 'critical' there is sometimes a need to step back and view them from the perspective of a community. A relatively minor assault on a member of a minority community could, for example, be the latest in a long series of racist incidents; how the police respond and the message that sends to the community is fundamental to developing and maintaining their relationships with families. Similarly *any* complaint of repeated victimization by *any* member of the community should be viewed by the police as potentially critical.

This chapter looks at the importance of family liaison in dealing with different types of potential critical incident, notably:

- missing persons;
- unexplained death;
- deaths abroad;
- other critical incidents abroad.

9.2 Missing Persons

In the UK many people are reported as 'missing from home' every year. Many, however, return home within a few hours of going missing. Some are adults who do not appear to be particularly vulnerable and who have made a conscious decision to go 'missing' and do not want to be traced by friends or relatives, either on a temporary or permanent basis. Some are young people who 'go missing' on a regular basis for whom there is or at least should be more concern even if they have always returned of their own volition up until that point, particularly when the reason for them going missing and/or risks associated with the place that they went to or people that they met is not known or well understood.

There are some cases in which there is grave concern as soon as a person is reported missing. What is it that raises the police response in these cases to 'critical'? It could, of course, be the age of the missing person (very young or very old). In these circumstances the missing person is considered vulnerable as a result of their inability to survive without appropriate care in any environment. People who have a learning disability or a physical disability, mental health issues or a serious illness are similarly likely to give cause for concern. Other aspects of the missing person's history may also contribute toward an assessment of the gravity of the situation. Such factors are likely to include:

- whether there is any obvious reason for the person to have gone missing;
- whether and in what circumstances they went missing before, including the circumstances of their return and any information regarding where they had been and who they had been with.

It is important to remember, however, that neither of these factors prevents a person from being vulnerable, particularly where age, disability, mental health or illness is an issue. It is rather the case that they might heighten concerns for the person, depending on the circumstances. For example, if the vulnerable person is known or believed to have previously associated with abusive or violent people when they went missing, concerns for their welfare will inevitably increase.

9.2.1 Missing persons: a police family liaison response

Police family liaison is an important consideration in every missing person scenario because in each case someone is very worried and may be looking to the police for a response, even if such a response is limited to good advice. This does not usually require the deployment of a specialist police family liaison officer but does require the engagement of appropriately skilled staff to liaise on behalf of the police with the person(s) reporting the person missing.

KEY POINT—POLICE FAMILY LIAISON RESPONSE TO MISSING PERSONS REPORTS

Police family liaison should be considered whenever a person is reported as missing. In most cases this does not require the deployment of a specialist family liaison officer because little more than good advice is needed. Whatever the situation, however, it does invariably merit the engagement of staff who have the necessary investigative and social skills to liaise effectively and sensitively with the family and/or other people who reported the person missing.

It is important to draw the distinction here between police family liaison and the deployment of specialist resources in a major or critical incident in the form of a family liaison officer. As is mentioned in the opening chapter, while liaison between police, families and communities takes place all the time it is important to understand that the deployment of a specially trained family liaison officer is a relatively rare event that is reserved for matters likely to require additional specialist skills. It would be a retrograde step in the police relationship with the community if the only people that could speak to them were specialists who had to be summoned from elsewhere. One way of looking at this is to think about every member of the police service who comes into contact with families in their line of duty as being, to some extent, a family liaison officer, from the most senior ranks to the most junior. Some cases, however, need additional specialist skills and it is in these cases that the deployment of a specialist family liaison officer should be carefully considered.

When Holly Wells and Jessica Chapman disappeared in Cambridgeshire on 4 August 2002 it quickly became a critical incident. This happened long before their bodies were found and the reason it was understood to be critical was because of a range of factors. These were two 10-year-old girls. They were not prone to going missing. There were no obvious factors in the family background or in events leading up to their disappearance that would suggest that the girls had run away or were in hiding. While it might appear obvious, the designation of this case as a 'critical incident' was actually due to experienced law enforcement practitioners carefully calculating a number of 'risk factors'. The modern police service needs to be tuned in to risk and critical incidents and, in the appropriate circumstances, the earliest possible deployment of a family liaison officer with a clear strategy is essential to securing vital early information and maintaining public confidence in policing.

Family liaison officers have no control over the type of case to which they are deployed. These decisions are rightly taken by SIOs, often with the assistance of family liaison coordinators and experienced family liaison officers who can provide advice whether a deployment is appropriate and how its benefits might be maximized. The UK police *Family Liaison Office Guidance* (ACPO, 2008) sets out some operating room in this regard for SIOs by stating that outside the core business of homicide, road death and mass fatality incidents, SIOs may consider the deployment of family liaison officers in an unexplained death or any other critical incident where police family liaison might enhance the effectiveness of the police response. It then gives the example of a missing person or a hate crime. These are clearly just examples out of any number of policing engagements that may become critical at some stage. It is important to understand early when something is becoming critical because it is very difficult to make up ground two weeks into an incident when forensic and CCTV opportunities are less likely still to be available.

9.2.2 **Missing persons: victimology**

There is a matter of urgency when making enquiries with family members and friends in 'missing from home' cases. In situations where there is grave concern, the development of a victimology can prove crucial to an investigation into the whereabouts of the missing person and the circumstances in which they went missing.

KEY POINT—VICTIMOLOGY FOR MISSING PERSONS

In situations where there is grave concern about a person who has been reported as missing the development of a victimology can prove crucial to the investigation into their whereabouts and the circumstances of them being missing.

It is sometimes over simplistic to ask a family member to think of places that the police might search for the missing person. It might be more productive to build up a profile of the person through victimology enquiries. For example, it may be useful to find out about their normal routine. A simple enquiry like this by a good interviewer is actually designed to discover things like:

- all known friends and associates;
- whether they work;
- where and when they work;
- how they get to work (the kind of transport used);
- which routes they take (finding out about routes can also be useful when identifying potential opportunities for capturing CCTV images);
- whether, where and with whom they socialize after work;
- how they spend their time, particularly if they do not work;
- whether, where and with whom they share any hobbies or pastimes;

- whether they have any strong opinions about anything;
- what kind of foods they like;
- any strange or interesting incidents that have occurred in the days, weeks and months leading up to the person going missing;
- whether they are able to access money;
- whether they know how to make travel arrangements.

This is not a definitive list and each victimology plan should be case dependent and focused on the individual and the circumstances. Having gathered this information it should be assessed and investigated further where appropriate. The result of these enquiries could be the need for another round of victimology questions to further develop the profile of the individual.

The potential to build up the missing person's profile is massive and requires a police family liaison officer to identify the most appropriate people to ask and then to conduct urgent interviews. Specialist family liaison officers can support this type of investigation to great effect. The advice and guidance of an interview adviser can make their contribution even more effective.

It would be unmanageable to try to do this with every missing person case though but there is room for the police service to embrace the 'victimology' principle in most investigations with the family liaison officer only being deployed in the ones that are becoming critical. Once deployed there really is no reason the comprehensive approach to understanding the victim's lifestyle cannot be achieved in a relatively short period of time.

It is obviously a time-consuming process but with good communication between family liaison officer and other members of an enquiry team, the information that the family liaison officer gathers can be communicated back and acted upon very quickly.

9.3 Unexplained Death

The term 'unexplained death' is used to refer to any case where the full circumstances of the death are yet to be fully investigated. This includes what would have been described in the past as 'suspected suicide'. No matter how obvious the interpretation of a scene appears to be, an investigation has to be carried out into the death and a report made to the coroner in England and Wales or the Procurator Fiscal if in Scotland. More generally the term 'unexplained death' is applied to a wide range of circumstances where the cause of death remains uncertain.

Other than during initial recruit training, police officers are given no extra training about delivering death notification. There has, however, been very little if any real criticism of police performance in this regard. It is a solemn message almost always delivered by a uniformed officer that gives it an 'official' and respectful gravitas.

It has been suggested that family liaison officers should not deliver a death notification because it will leave the family with bad feelings toward them but

> **Example—unexplained death**
>
> Police are called to a popular beauty spot where a motor vehicle is found partially submerged in water at the end of a track at the bottom of a short but steep incline. The male driver and the female passenger are both dead. Did these deaths occur as a result of a dreadful accident or misadventure, a 'suicide pact', was one murdered by the other before the other committed suicide, was the driver under the influence of drink or drugs, was the driver trying to control his passenger who was under the influence of drink or drugs, did a domestic altercation take place causing the driver to be distracted? One could generate endless hypotheses as to the cause of these deaths but such matters are best decided upon by the coroner on the basis of what is established during a thorough investigation. The circumstances surrounding a death such as those referred to in this example are likely to be referred to as 'unexplained' until the coroner makes a decision about them.

there is no research to support this suggestion. The reason family liaison officers do not usually deliver a death message is actually a logistical rather than a philosophical one: family liaison officers need to be briefed, plan their initial contact with the family and their deployment needs to be risk-assessed before they visit the family home; while this can be done fairly quickly, death notifications are important and *must never be delayed*. One of the worst things that can happen to the police/family relationship is for the media to break the news of a death before the police have made official contact with the family. Some of the cases that have turned into critical incidents have started very badly as a result of this and it is very difficult to repair the trust and confidence that is so essential to the relationship between the family and the family liaison officer.

The language that the police use when dealing with bereaved relatives is extremely important. For many years the words 'road traffic accident' were used to describe a myriad of events involving motor vehicles and the death of human beings. Today this is no longer acceptable terminology because it implies a judgment by the police as to what has happened before the completion of a full investigation.

It is essential that police officers understand that the language they use can have an impact on the family. Families expect professionalism from the agencies involved with them at this most difficult of times.

In cases where suicide seems to be the most obvious conclusion, it is essential to avoid conveying any opinion to the family. It is a very difficult time for a family and suicide can often bring on great feelings of guilt about a family member. Even in the most obvious, clear-cut cases, families will often look for any answer other than suicide. The police service must investigate all unexplained deaths without expressing an opinion. It is essential that they maintain an investigative mindset throughout the investigation.

Example: terminology

At a conference for families and victims some years ago a woman in the audience asked the question to the whole room.

> My beautiful daughters were waiting at a bus stop one evening when two young men who had been drinking decided to race each other in their unsafe and uninsured cars. One of them mounted the kerb and killed my daughters. *The question I have is this; was it right for the police officer to report to me in the first instance that they had died in an accident?*

She went on to describe her daughters' deaths as having been caused by a road homicide.

At the time of writing it is still fairly unusual for a family liaison officer to be deployed in a case of unexplained death. There may, however, be a need for some investigation to be done at the early stages of an enquiry and it is in this early stage that a family liaison officer could be extremely valuable. Establishing some 'victimology' from family and friends will assist in building up an eventual case file for the coroner or the Procurator Fiscal. The statement of principle for police family liaison (see chapter 2) refers to 'death of a human being, where there is a police investigation'; unexplained deaths clearly fall into this category. It may be a short-term deployment but it is still very important in maintaining the trust and confidence in any investigative process.

9.4 Deaths Abroad

The British police service has no jurisdiction when a UK citizen is killed abroad; the police in the country where the death occurred are responsible for the investigation. There are some occasions, however, when a request can be made to a UK force to take some investigative action either on behalf of the police in the host country or on behalf of the Foreign and Commonwealth Office.

A family liaison officer deployment in these circumstances should only be considered if there is an investigative purpose. This should be to either collect investigative information or intelligence from the family and friends or to assist in the identification of the dead person. If these conditions are met then the same rules apply about the family liaison officer deployment as they do in the UK, including:

- risk assessment;
- full operational briefing;
- a written family liaison strategy;
- local line management and supervision.

It should be noted that the cost of deploying a family liaison officer for these purposes in the UK usually rests with the force with geographic responsibility for the area in which the family reside.

Family liaison officers in the UK cannot be 'managed' either by the foreign force or the Foreign and Commonwealth Office. It is reasonable to suggest, therefore, that an SIO and a family liaison coordinator should also be involved when a family liaison officer is deployed in these circumstances. The involvement of an SIO and a family liaison coordinator is important because they have to develop and manage the family liaison strategy, review and manage the risk assessment, and describe and implement the exit strategy. They also have to supervise the family liaison officer logs and any other written work that the family liaison officer produces. Family liaison officers and their managers need to liaise and work closely with the appropriate desk officer at the Foreign and Commonwealth Office.

The deployment of a family liaison officer in instances of deaths abroad is often quite complex because the police in the UK are not automatically given all the necessary information about the investigation from the foreign force. When they are given information it often arrives 'out of hours' because of time differences and it may need to be interpreted accurately before it is shared. It is, therefore, imperative that the family liaison officer tries to avoid giving the family unrealistic expectations for the release of information; the flow of information from the investigation to the family is likely to be much slower than it is in the case of an investigation in the UK.

The family liaison officer should never attempt to contact foreign police forces directly without the express agreement of the Foreign and Commonwealth Office. The Foreign and Commonwealth Office has absolute primacy for UK matters abroad and if a good partnership is to be developed between police and the Foreign and Commonwealth Office all parties must adhere to strict operating procedures that acknowledge this position.

9.5 **Other Critical Incidents Abroad**

In addition to instances of death abroad, the police in the UK are sometimes asked to take investigative action either on behalf of the police in a foreign country or the Foreign and Commonwealth Office as a result of a serious offence that has taken place abroad. In these circumstances it might be argued that the very nature of some incidents that take place on foreign soil can give rise to a critical incident in the UK because they have a significant impact on a victim or a family that resides in the UK. For example, when Madeleine McCann disappeared in Portugal in May 2007 the media interest was extremely high around the family home in Leicester. It therefore became necessary for the police in Leicestershire to make some provision to offer assistance to the investigation in Portugal. This has happened in a number of cases, such as when a number of UK citizens were taken hostage in Iraq. These are sensitive cases that require a very tight control of information.

Critical incidents can, therefore, affect the police service even when they have no direct involvement with the investigation from which they arise. When a case has a significant media interest the risk can increase.

9.6 Chapter Summary

This chapter has considered the contribution that family liaison can make to an investigation into a critical incident. To this end, it has described a critical incident as a situation in which the police response to it is likely to have a significant impact on the confidence of the victim or their family, or the wider community. The early deployment of a family liaison officer can be of great benefit in circumstances where an investigative response that centres on the family is required. Such a deployment should also involve the appointment of an SIO and a family liaison coordinator to develop and manage the family liaison strategy and the family liaison officer.

This chapter has sought to illustrate the kinds of issue involved in the deployment of family liaison officers in critical incidents by considering their role in connection with missing persons, unexplained deaths, deaths abroad and other critical incidents abroad.

NOTES

NOTES

NOTES

10

Family Liaison Officer Welfare

10.1 Introduction

The activity of delivering police family liaison is rarely anything less than intense. This applies to the families and to the police officer(s) working with them. While the family liaison officers should have been specially selected for their professional skills, it does not always make them immune from absorbing some of the trauma that the families they work with are going through.

It is essential that supervisors and line managers of family liaison officers know their staff and are aware of any personal issues that could interfere with their ability to work on a particular case. Due to the immediacy of a family liaison officer's deployment in an investigation into a death, it is not always easy for a supervisor to conduct an interview with them to assess their suitability for any given case. Police forces should, therefore, try to reach a position where a system is in place that promotes welfare provision for family liaison officers at all times, whether they are deployed or not.

The purpose of this chapter is to examine positive methods of looking after staff. In doing this, reference will be made to research conducted by Dr Anne Eyre, 'Family Liaison: Making a Difference' (unpublished paper). Dr Eyre is a sociologist and independent consultant specializing in stress, trauma and disaster management.

10.2 Getting it Right

It seems reasonable to suggest that if we really want to know about the difficulties involved in doing a job then we should ask the people doing it. If we create the right environment and they trust us, they will make sure that we know what works and what does not. The first major point to make here is, therefore, that practitioners need to have some means of communicating their concerns to line managers. This amounts to more than organizing a training day that is opened by a senior manager once a year; it involves having a channel of communication that is open all the time so that feedback can be given and received.

In the early days of police family liaison there were few protocols in place to protect against and prevent 'burn out' among family liaison officers. As the years have gone on family liaison officers themselves have helped to design and develop operating systems by being prepared to give honest and sometimes painful feedback to managers and policy makers. The second major point here is that someone has to hear what family liaison officers are saying, understand and evaluate it and have the power and ability to act upon it. The value of providing the people who actually do the work, in this instance family liaison officers, with an opportunity to communicate with their managers and to influence the future development of the discipline is best illustrated by the debriefing that followed the investigation into the Ladbroke Grove rail disaster.

10.3 The Ladbroke Grove Rail Disaster Debriefing

A debriefing took place following the Ladbroke Grove rail disaster on 3 November 1999. The written objectives of the debriefing were to identify :

- what in the coordination and delivery of family liaison services did and did not work and what with hindsight might have been done differently;
- practical issues of concern for family liaison officers and collate suggestions for their future, the police service and family liaison policy;
- future training needs;
- support mechanisms required to facilitate family liaison officers performing the role;
- models for effective management structures required to coordinate family liaison officers in major disasters.

Ladbroke Grove was a new situation for family liaison officers because it was the first time they had been deployed to a major disaster. It follows that this debrief was the first of its kind for family liaison officers, and that the people developing this new investigative discipline were taking account of feedback from the staff from the start.

One hundred and eleven family liaison officers were used in the aftermath of this disaster and they were all brought back together to take part in this debrief. During their deployment it had become necessary to break them up into teams with a line manager or coordinator overseeing the work of roughly 10 family liaison officers each. Each team had its own debrief in the morning before coming back together for a plenary session. In each room with the teams there was a facilitator, a note taker and a member of the Occupational Health Department of the Metropolitan Police Service. The teams of family liaison officers were consulted about the process, including who should be present during the debriefing. All the comments were captured by a note taker and recorded without identifying the person who made them.

There was no written policy or guidance for family liaison anywhere in the UK at this time. While work had begun to develop guidance in various parts of the country, a national corpus of best practice was not readily accessible. It was, therefore, important to ask the people who were actually delivering the role on behalf of the police service, the family liaison officers themselves.

10.4 Points Raised During the Ladbroke Grove Debriefing

Some very significant points were raised by the officers during the Ladbroke Grove debriefing, which went on to shape the family liaison model that exists in the UK now. These points were as follows:

- Communication issues are paramount. Family liaison officers need to be able to communicate with the rest of the investigation team. It is not acceptable to deploy staff to such an intense area of business without the means to keep in touch with their colleagues. The organization needs to be in a position to issue a mobile telephone to family liaison officers whenever they are deployed. It is not appropriate to ask family liaison officers to give their own personal telephone details to a family. This changes the nature of the police/family relationship and makes implementing an exit strategy far more difficult.
- Local line managers inadvertently add to the pressure on family liaison officers when they ask when they will return to their normal duty. While it is accepted that local line managers have their own priorities, someone other than the family liaison officer should be deputed to liaise with them to explain what their staff are doing and give them an idea when they might expect them back.
- The team structure that was set up for family liaison officers working on the Ladbroke Grove rail disaster worked well and helped the officers to feel supported by their team leader. The obvious conclusion to draw from this was that there was a need to create a specialist position, which became that of family liaison coordinator. As a direct result of this debriefing, the role of family liaison coordinator was introduced by the Metropolitan Police Service. This role is now nationally accepted and every UK police force has family liaison coordinators. The initial job description that was drafted for a family liaison coordinator was that their role was to 'create an environment whereby the family liaison officer can successfully deliver the SIO or SIM's strategy'. This includes discussing the nature of the family liaison officer's deployment with SIOs and their line managers, including the issues raised above relating to how long they are likely to be away from their everyday duties and to negotiate a 'back-to-work plan' that eases the family liaison officer back into their everyday routine in a manner that does not have an adverse impact on them. Anecdotally some family liaison officers talked about having been deployed on this disaster for long hours in a very intense environment only to find on their return to their normal work that they were on a week of night shifts without a day off. So it was important to hear what the family liaison officers were saying about their experience and to act upon it.
- A number of comments were made to the effect that it was an advantage to have two family liaison officers deployed together to each family; not only on a professional level but on a personal one as well. There can be little doubt that one of the factors that can sometimes adversely affect a family liaison officer is the feeling that sometimes occurs of isolation from the rest of the investigation team. The nature of the role sometimes means that they are spending periods of time working within the family home. Some of the work takes time and requires lengthy interviews with family members. This can sometimes lead to the family liaison officers being separated from the rest of

the investigative team for a lengthy period of time. If this occurs and the family liaison officer is working alone it is likely to be detrimental to the welfare of the individual. As a direct consequence of this, the Metropolitan Police Service made sure that its family liaison guidelines recommended that family liaison officers should be deployed in pairs. This was later incorporated into national guidelines in the UK as best practice.

- Family liaison officers pointed out that relationships with other agencies are one of the keys to success. This is extremely important during a mass fatality deployment when there are a number of agencies involved in delivering 'humanitarian assistance' to people affected by the disaster. It is important that effort by different agencies is not duplicated. The experience of multi-agency working led to a clearer definition for the role of the family liaison officer by the police in the UK. Even at this early stage, there were concerns that police family liaison officers could be dragged into areas beyond their expertise. Many of the families praised the family liaison officers after Ladbroke Grove, but some of the functions that they ended up performing would, perhaps, have been better delivered by another agency that had been trained and funded to do that role. The role of the police family liaison officer has to be clearly defined for the family, and the family liaison officer has to be supported in exiting the police/family relationship when the extent of the police responsibility and capability has been exhausted. All police forces in the UK now take part in multi-agency training, and there is a national steering group made up of support agencies who advise the UK police about their relationships with families in the event of sudden and tragic death that requires a police investigation. The benefit of relationships with other agencies is that it ensures that police family liaison officers do not deal with matters for which they have no training. It also helps to make sure that the family liaison officer exits at the appropriate time because someone else is there to assist the family in the longer term. All police family liaison coordinators should make sure that they have relationships in place locally that will assist family liaison officers in the delivery of their role.
- Family liaison officers asked for a peer-support network with regular team meetings. Debriefs among peers has continued to be popular with family liaison officers. There is something to be said for being given the opportunity to discuss issues with like-minded people or at least people who will understand the context. This has been written into national guidance. It is recommended that family liaison coordinators run at least one training day a year for current family liaison officers. Time should be set aside at these days for family liaison officers to discuss emerging issues that need to be addressed. It is empowering for practitioners to know that someone is interested in their issues and is prepared to take action to resolve them.
- Family liaison officers requested that there should be easy access to occupational health services. Culturally this has always been difficult for the police service. Officers often feel compelled not to show vulnerability when dealing

with difficult issues. Things have, however, moved on since the role of family liaison officer was first established. It is every officer's responsibility to speak up when there are matters that may affect their performance in the role. National family liaison guidance has made this much easier by recommending that referral to occupational health should be compulsory for those performing the role of family liaison officer. This should take place at least once a year and should also be considered when someone has been involved with a particularly difficult deployment. Making this a compulsory aspect of being a family liaison officer takes away any stigma that could be attached in a policing organization to asking for help. Leaders have a major part to play in the success of an occupational health strategy—first of all in the maintenance of a programme that ensures that nobody is missed and, secondly, by organizing and attending group debriefs with the team. Occupational health departments should be involved with the selection of potential family liaison officers, their training and ongoing welfare. It is essential that family liaison coordinators have a working group for family liaison within their force that has representation from occupational health.

- Family liaison officers requested that a service protocol or policy was written on family liaison. It was thus the practitioners themselves who first recognized the need for policy. This is significant because it indicates a sign of the maturity and intelligence that was beginning to develop among practitioners. Often in large organizations policy is a top-down process intended to ensure that staff are adhering to a management plan. In family liaison, however, policy evolved as more of a bottom-up process, because it was forced to adapt as it was used from one crisis to another. Allowing practitioners to take part in the design of policy and guidance has helped family liaison officers and family liaison coordinators to feel involved in the development of their respective roles. Family liaison practitioners must always have local, regional and national representation that feeds into policy, training and development of the family liaison role nationally.

It is evident from the Ladbroke Grove rail disaster debriefing in the early days of family liaison how important it is to hear what practitioners have to say.

10.5 'Family Liaison: Making a Difference': a Paper by Dr Anne Eyre

In March 2007 Dr Anne Eyre undertook a piece of research with police family liaison practitioners and in doing so asked them the following questions:

- In your view what do you find is the most rewarding aspect of your work as a family liaison officer?
- In your view what is the most challenging aspect of your work as a family liaison officer?

Examples—rewarding aspects:

'Helping people, being at the hub of major crime, knowing that you are doing a worthwhile job' (crime/homicide family liaison officer, nine years' experience)

'Helping families with understanding the role of the police during the investigations of fatal road traffic collisions' (roads policing family liaison officer, 18 months' experience)

'Privilege of working with families who are raw in feelings but able to conduct an intense investigation at this difficult time and feeding all info back to major incident room' (crime/homicide family liaison officer, two and a half years' experience)

'Very rewarding to assist bereaved people through the investigative process' (crime/homicide family liaison officer, three years' experience)

'Two simple ideas – helping victims and being an effective investigating police officer' (roads policing family liaison officer, two years' experience)

- What, if anything, would make it easier to fulfil your role as a family liaison officer?
- What piece of advice would you give to a new family liaison officer based on your experience of this role?

Some of the points made by practitioners in response to these questions are reported in the boxes that follow. These points should be considered by family liaison offcers and those who manage them.

These are good answers from family liaison officers that show a commitment to their own professionalism and a good understanding of the importance of the family to the investigative process. It is important to understand, however, that the family liaison officers feel it is *rewarding* to play a full part in the investigative process. Concerns for family liaison officers and their welfare arise when they feel detached or isolated from the investigative process.

Example—challenges

'On occasions there can be a three or four way pull ... despite being aware of your own needs and meeting these it can be difficult to reconcile (them) without feeling guilty' (roads policing family liaison officer, four years' experience)

This is a very honest comment from a family liaison officer. It is essential that family liaison officers are aware of the impact that a deployment can have on them. It is also very important that the impact on family liaison officers is recognized by those supervising and advising them. There will be times when family liaison officers have to take time off and attend to their own personal lives. They must be allowed to do this and not to feel guilty about it. This is another clear reason for the role of family liaison coordinator to exist. The specific danger of not taking time out when needed is that the family liaison officer will become exhausted and potentially make bad decisions. Good supervision can and must prevent this.

Example—making the family liaison role easier

'(It is) crucial to have an SIO with full understanding of the role and not be earmarked as tea and sympathy' (crime/homicide family liaison officer, three years' experience)

'There are times when the family liaison officer can be forgotten in relation to the hard work they conduct. This recognition is largely unseen by supervision of the higher ranks who are concerned only with figures and statistics' (roads policing family liaison officer, three years' experience)

Greater recognition by supervisors and colleagues was the factor most commonly identified by family liaison officers as being likely to make their work easier. There is often very good feedback from families, which is appreciated by the officers, but this is not always reflected in how the police service manages its family liaison officers. One common misunderstanding is that the family liaison officer is a provider of tea and sympathy. There is a need by family liaison coordinators to 'market' the family liaison officers' role inside the organization. This is an ongoing task because the problem appears to have been in existence since the introduction of police family liaison in its current form. It would be fair to say, however, that the forces where the morale of family liaison officers is highest are the forces with effective family liaison leadership.

10.6 Involving Family Liaison Officers in the Future

As suggested earlier in this chapter, the family liaison officer training days are important as an opportunity for family liaison officers to exchange ideas and learning with each other. This has the effect of keeping their knowledge up to date and allows family liaison officers to spend time with like-minded peers who understand the work that they do.

A good way of promoting a commitment to family liaison is to invite other appropriate people along to family liaison officer training days. This might include SIOs, potential recruits to family liaison roles or people from other agencies who may work with families following the death of a loved one.

The final part of Dr Anne Eyre's research paper asked family liaison officers the following question: 'What advice would you give a new family liaison officer?' The responses to this question were as follows:

Example—advice to give to new family liaison officers

1. Be clear about your role/responsibilities with the family and set boundaries of contact.
2. Treat the next-of-kin how you would like to be treated, be honest and most of all human!
3. Be truthful at all times with the family even if the information you have to give is upsetting.
4. Keep in constant liaison with the senior investigating officer.
5. Keep the family updated as much as possible without delay. What might seem trivial to you could be the most important piece of information the family could hear.
6. Recognize your own strengths and weaknesses. Be prepared to talk and seek support.
7. Keep your sense of humour.
8. Take your rest days.
9. Listen to other family liaison officers' experience.
10. Remember, this may be the first time the family have met a police officer, and the impression you leave will be a lasting one.

These points were all made by serving police family liaison officers: who better to reflect on their role?

10.7 Chapter Summary

The theme of this chapter has been about looking after the welfare of family liaison officers and other family liaison practitioners. A checklist for making sure this happens might look like this:

- user-friendly written guidelines that practitioners are familiar with and understand;
- effective management structures;
- good training with regular updates;
- communication structures that support the family liaison officer (the family liaison officer needs to be heard and listened to);
- a mandatory occupational health system in force that needs to be stringently managed;
- healthy relationships with other appropriate agencies.

If police forces can achieve the points on this checklist they should have a foundation for success. It is important to remember, however, that this is only the beginning; systems have to be maintained, staff need to be looked after, new people need to be encouraged and mentored through the system. The need to be ready is constant—whether it is the high demand for family liaison officers in road deaths, the complex and tragic deaths that occur through homicide or the enduring threat of terrorist attacks or other tragic events that incur heavy loss of life. There can be no complacency in policing about a role that many seem to think is the finished article: there is much yet to achieve in this area.

It should also be remembered that the responsibility for the delivery of police family liaison rests with the police service itself, not with the family liaison officers. Police family liaison officers carry out this invaluable role, often on top of their day job, on behalf of the police service.

It is, therefore, the case that no family liaison officer can be truly successful unless they are supervised, resourced and supported by their police force throughout their career.

NOTES

NOTES

NOTES

Index

20082134R00096

Printed in Poland
by Amazon Fulfillment
Poland Sp. z o.o., Wrocław